Teaching Belly Dance
By Sara Shrapnell

Teaching Belly Dance
by Sara Shrapnell

Hoffman Gifford Publishing

Hoffman Gifford Publishing
Teaching Belly Dance
Sara Shrapnell
Copyright ©2014 Sara Shrapnell
All rights reserved

Copyeditor: Kristi Hein
Cover Design: Chi Chan
Interior Design: Dawn Devine ~ Davina of Ibexa Press
Cover Photography: K. Shrapnell
Interior Photography: Alisha Westerfeld unless otherwise specified
Additional Photography:
    Donna Ovenden pp 69, 71
    Jesse Stanbridge p 68

Readers should consult experts in their local area for up to date medical, legal and tax advice before setting up their business or teaching in any form

If you would like to do any of the above, please seek permission via our web site:
    www.TeachingBellyDance.com

ISBN 0615980848

This book is dedicated to Sandra Day, my mother and Poppy, my daughter. One day we will all dance together.

Table of Contents

FOREWORD

The book you are holding in your hands is a comprehensive guide for anyone who aspires to become a belly dance instructor. Absolutely everything – the obvious and the more esoteric things that never even crossed your mind- about teaching this beautiful art is covered. There are sections on lesson plans, suggested warm ups and cool downs for different skill levels, and pertinent info on studio or instructor finances and book keeping. Sara Shrapnell delves deep into the psychology of the many and varied types of learners, and details methodologies that will encourage students to grasp technique and concepts and to excel. There are even sections on dealing with somewhat abstract- but extremely important- topics such as encouraging newer dancers to emote during performances, or how to handle problem students.

Many years ago, when she was still living in England, Sara Shrapnell and Emma Pyke hosted me for a workshop at the Let's Belly Dance Studio. Sara's sparkling eyes and bubbly personality immediately struck me. She was also a lovely dancer, and had obviously very well promoted. The workshop was absolutely packed, and I was surprised and impressed to learn that the many dancers in attendance were all their students. They were extremely well trained, with competent technique in their various levels. But what really stood out was the way Sara's pupils related to her; though she was amiable and fun, she emanated a gentle authority in the way that only a natural leader can- and it was clear that every woman in the room not only respected but revered her.

It's this easy finesse-combined with her knowledge and years of experience- that makes this book so valuable. Teaching Belly Dance is written beautifully and is so thoughtful and thorough that every teacher- no matter how experienced- ought to keep a copy on hand for reference!

Princess Farhana

ABOUT THE AUTHOR

Sara Shrapnell attended her first belly dance class in 1992, with the aim of toning up and regaining her fitness after the birth of her son. Instead, she discovered a dance form that pulled at her heart much more than the ballet and disco lessons of her childhood had done. She met some amazing people and fell in love with the UK belly dance scene.

Her weekly class soon turned into two, four, and then six classes a week, first with Tina Hobin and then with Afra Al-Kahira. In 2000 she studied the Al Kahira School of Middle Eastern Dance (ASMED) teacher training course, which includes study with City & Guilds (a leading UK vocational education organization) to gain qualifications in adult education, as well as belly dance–based learning.

Sara took on established classes and approached local gyms and councils, quickly expanding her teaching to twelve classes a week. She graduated from ASMED in 2003 and continued to work within the organization to mentor other teachers as they studied the course. Together with Emma Pyke she set up Mersin, a professional troupe comprising local teachers and performers. She also directed a number of student troupes, including Nashida Abla and a Tribal Fusion group, who performed in a huge variety of venues. In addition to hosting a popular "Day of Dance," which ran two or three times a year for ten years, Sara planned many stage shows, workshops, and hafla for her students. For five years she was a member of the Wessex Arabic Dance Network committee, helping to bring high-quality events to the wider community.

In 2011 Sara closed her UK classes and moved to the San Francisco Bay Area to continue her studies in all styles of belly dance. Here she has rediscovered the art of starting a business from scratch, the joys of business bureaucracy, and the pitfalls of the language shared by British and Americans. She is currently teaching at a gym, for the cities of Pleasanton and Dublin, and as an independent contractor at a dance studio.

Her classes are known for their humor, detailed breakdowns, and cultural context. She adapts her lessons to suit the dancers according to their needs and aims. Students who have studied with Sara have gone on to teach and perform in all styles of belly dance, and many have made their living through performance or teaching. She continues to support dancers and teachers through one-on-one mentoring and online and private lessons.

Sara is the proud mother of three and has also written a novel.

HOW TO USE THIS BOOK

This book is aimed at those who are new to teaching belly dance or who are looking to start teaching in the future, be they professional dancers, dedicated students, teacher assistants, or class leaders. It is assumed that readers have an excellent understanding of the basic moves and some depth in their chosen specialization. This is not primarily a book on what to teach, so much as how to teach belly dance.

I believe that books are a poor way to learn movement, and with an excellent range of DVDs on the market, everyone should be able to learn how to dance many different styles along with all the basic moves of belly dance. For this reason I decided not to fill this book with instructions on how to do moves. Of course, working with a teacher is an even better way to learn, and if you have only had the chance to work from DVDs, you will need to take workshops or attend intensive training before you can move on to sharing those skills with others.

I have included a variety of different ways to teach the basic moves, and although belly dance doesn't have a worldwide naming system, I have crafted my descriptions to make it easy to understand which moves I mean.

I also wanted this book to be useful to teachers in all styles of belly dance, not to simply push my own dance style. The key moves are what will make your classes "belly dance," but your own styling, accent, dance skills, and history are what will make your classes uniquely yours. I have included lots of instructions on how to write your own term and lesson plans, so that you can share your own style at a pace that suits you and your students.
In addition to lesson planning, I have included practical tips on how to set up and promote classes, how to deal with students, and how to keep up with your own training. I have shared my thoughts about the different learning styles, classroom planning, student performances, and event planning. I hope that together they give you the confidence to glide onto the next stage of your teaching.

I have also included practical projects to help you research and prepare for teaching in your own area. You can work through them in the order in which they are presented here, or you may prefer to skip around to chapters that interest you.

I may occasionally repeat myself in case readers have missed a particularly important point in an earlier chapter.

I have also made the decision to refer to both the student and the teacher most often as "she." While I know many amazing male dancers and teachers, I feel that referring to everyone as "he or she" would become tiresome for the reader. Belly dance is still primarily a female-dominated realm; my writing reflects that.

Please note that all opinions in this book are my own, and you may well know – or be! – a greater expert in these topics. I have studied belly dance for more than twenty years, but I know I have only scratched the surface, and I apologize for any mistakes I have made. This book is my advice to new teachers, and, as with any advice, you may take what is helpful to you and leave what is not.

I wish you many happy years of enjoyable, rewarding, and profitable belly dance classes.

Sara Shrapnell

ARE YOU READY TO TEACH BELLY DANCE?

You have been dancing for a few years now, taking lessons and workshops. You have been thinking about becoming a teacher, so much so that you bought this book. How do you know if you are ready? Is it the right choice for you? Do you have something interesting to teach others, and will students flock to you for lessons? Can you make a living at this? Will the students like you? How do you set up a business, organize your lesson plan, and find a great venue? Where do you start?

First, realize that good dancing and good teaching are two very different skills. Some people are excellent at both, but most of us are not that lucky. Just being a great dancer won't make you a fantastic dance teacher, but conversely, if you love belly dance but not your performance opportunities, you could well find your calling as a belly dance teacher.

Teachers need to be people focused, show endless patience, be well organized and experts in their subject. Does that sound like you?

As a dancer you have learned the moves and how to put them together in a way that is pleasing to your audience. Can you now develop those skills so that the moves look beautiful on different body shapes? Can you keep your students safe and happy at the same time? Can you make the drills interesting and the choreographies intuitive? I may be biased, but I do think that teaching belly dance is one of the best jobs in the world; however, like so many other things, you'll get out of it in proportion to what you put in. If your passion for belly dance is so great that you are bursting to share the joy with others, then we have a great starting point.

There is no ideal length of time to have been studying belly dance before you venture into teaching, but you need to have ascended through the ranks in your teacher's classes, completing beginner's (not jumping into a more advanced class too quickly), intermediate, and advanced level classes. You should have covered a number of different styles of belly dance; be skilled with veil, stick, and finger cymbals; have learned group and solo choreographies and also improvised; know some of the history of belly dance (not simply a myth or two); be confident with the drum solo; and have some performing experience.

Not all teachers will be able to cover all these subjects for you, so you need to attend workshops not only in subjects you love but also to fill gaps in your education. You do not have to be an expert in ATS, shaabi, baladi, modern and classical Egyptian, Gothic, Nubian, Al Jeel, American Cabaret, Lebanese, khaleggi, Turkish folk and cabaret, and all the fusion styles in order to teach beginners, but you need to be able to identify the music, talk about the history and famous names, and give a thirty-second performance if a student asks about it. Many dancers specialize in a particular form of belly dance, but as a teacher your knowledge must be broad. Depth is a wonderful thing, and it will help you as you move on to teaching more advanced students and workshops, but now is the time to make sure you have wide-ranging belly dance knowledge.

Practical Tip:

Make a list of all the different styles of belly dance that you know. Pick out a piece of music for each style and dance to each in front of a mirror for one minute. Check your dance styling changes for each type of belly dance. Do an internet search and pick out a suitable costume for each style. Study leading performers and their influences. Now make a handout for your students with some ideas about a variety of dance styles. You may want to do a simple one, with half a dozen styles, for beginners, and a more complex one, covering everything, for your advanced students. Each time you think your list is complete, search other dancers' sites, look at lists of workshops offered at events, or surf the available videos. When you discover a style you don't know much about, try to take a workshop with an expert. There is no end to this learning process! Keep updating your handout so that you are reminded of how much you already know. Finally, make sure your handout has your contact details and a copyright notice on the bottom.

I also suggest you return to local beginner classes and look again at beginner workshops. Often, in our rush to move ahead with dance skills, we miss important foundational elements. Even a lesson covering moves that you are strong in can teach you new skills and nuances, either as a dancer or as a teacher. Does your teacher break down the moves enough? Does she wait for a positive response? Does she adjust each dancer? Or is she negative in her feedback? Is the warm-up long enough? Is it fun? Does she chat off topic or stay focused? Are the students relaxed? How does your balance shift during the moves? What tempo suits your dancing? Does the teacher use different move names from those you use?

Make notes after the class about what worked and what didn't work. Her teaching style may be very different from yours, but we can all learn from each other.

If you are taking a trip or going on vacation, ask if you can drop in on a class with a local teacher or attend a workshop. Your hometown teaching style may have a very different feel from that of other teachers. Buy, rent, or borrow belly dance videos of all levels and observe the teaching styles. Teaching on video is a different skill from teaching live, but each will give you a flavor of what works for that teacher. Don't be afraid to admit that some of your basic moves are a bit off or that you tend to unconsciously go to an arm frame too often. Now is the time to perfect your basic moves, before you are faced with a room full of students who are all reflecting your bad habits back at you.

All of this learning is going to cost you money; indeed, the reason many dancers want to start teaching is to help cover their learning costs! Sad to say, very few teachers of belly dance can make a full-time living at it, but many use teaching to fund the workshops and events they want to attend. If your aim is to make a living from belly dance, you should understand that, as is true for most small businesses, it could take a couple of years to break even, and you will need some considerable savings or another job to tide you over until that happens. Most teachers start with one class to supplement their full-time job, with the aim of adding classes until they can go part time with their day job and then moving slowly to teaching belly dance full time. It is good to have a one-year, a five-year, and maybe even a ten-year plan to give yourself something to aim for. Also, do a quick spreadsheet of how much your dancing costs you each year. You may frighten yourself, but this will give you a realistic idea of how much you will need to make in profit to cover your dance costs.

Practical Tip:

Stop reading now and write down what your belly dancing has cost you in the last twelve months. List everything: classes, workshops, costumes, music, events, DVDs, belts and veils and earrings. Now create a dream list of what you would spend if you won the lottery. You are allowed five minutes to surf the $1,000 costumes, international week-long intensives, and flights to see your favorite dancer perform. Then you have to come back and read this book to see how (or if) you are going to get there.

Many of us fall into teaching belly dance when our teacher moves away or a subgroup of students wants to focus on a different style. This can be daunting for the new teacher, especially if that change happens fast. I think that students appreciate knowing that you consider yourself a "teacher in training," and it is perfectly possible to learn on the job, as long as you can keep your students safe and take your time to build up a student base. Set yourself the aim of becoming a great teacher within a year, and focus your dance training on that objective. Having an established class to start with is a huge bonus, and if you ask for the students' help you can learn a lot from their feedback.

However, be aware that at some point you need to transition from being their classmate to being their teacher. Consider taking an adult teaching exam, a course in teaching aerobics, or something similar so that you can involve them in your development but still have a date set when you will receive your certificate and officially become the class teacher. The students will appreciate your commitment to them and your strong leadership. You might also consider taking one of the specialist courses in teaching belly dance; many of these are excellent, but they usually take a few years. For a quick transition from classmate to teacher in your students' eyes, I suggest a week long intensive or weekend event. That is not to say I don't recommend a course focused on training you to be a belly dance teacher. Every teacher can learn from one of these courses, plus the networking can prove amazingly useful. They are

a good way to not only learn about teaching belly dance but also meet others who are doing the same, share problems with those who have already solved them, and keep focused on deadlines for your own development. Each course will have its own benefits and drawbacks. Some people prefer to work online, while others like a monthly or quarterly intensive. Some courses are run by one person; others come through team collaboration. You will need to look into what would work best for you, as they are a big financial investment and you don't want to drop out halfway through the course. Perhaps you need to add completing one of them to your one-year or five-year plan.

If you do find yourself unexpectedly taking over as the class leader, then consider asking another teacher you respect to mentor you for a year or so. Make it clear early on what your needs are and agree on a fair price. Some teachers will send you their term and lesson plans and give you a few hours of instruction in how to teach that course. Others will come and visit your class once a month or once a quarter and set you up with activities to focus on for the next few weeks. With email and video chat, it is becoming easier to coteach your class with someone more experienced. If you are using a mentor, be sure to let your students know immediately. They will feel cheated if they find out later. I also suggest that you don't simply learn from videos and use that as a basis to teach your class. Your students will inevitably find out, and if you simply follow the video, you won't be tailoring your classes to your students. From time to time we all say "Here is a great move I learned from a workshop/video with Miss Famous Dancer," and that helps the students to see that you are constantly learning, but be careful not to become a clone. Your individual style of belly dance and teaching is what will attract students to learn from you.

WHAT IS YOUR STYLE OF TEACHING?

When setting up your first class, it's a good idea to have a nice, clear view of what you want to teach and how. Your plan may be altered by the range of students who attend, but it's a starting point. Do you want to be fitness focused? Or will your classes be holistic? Are you looking to form a performance group? Or would you love to run a beautiful drum circle? Are you going to be a stickler for good technique? Are you going to teach Egyptian style only? Or do you want to manage a team of restaurant dancers? Will your classes include finger cymbals? Do you want to be a sister studio to a form of tribal dance, or do you want to create a new fusion style of belly dance?

Practical Tip:
Imagine your dream class in five years' time. What kind of students do you want to attract? Now is the time to put down the roots for that class.

TIMING IT RIGHT

Before we discuss where you are going to teach, we have to consider when, and for how long. The perfect time for your class will depend on where you live and the type of students you want to attract.

The first time slot is the before-work market, which is often popular with dancers who also take yoga or who have built the habit of working out first thing in the morning through attending sports training or running. These students want a convenient location with easy parking and will favor a location with showers and a changing area with mirrors and hair dryers.

The next group you might want to attract is those who have time for a class during the day. They tend to be stay-at-home parents, the early retired and retired, and those who work from home or have flexible working hours. If you can find a studio near a school, you may be able to catch the morning school run; otherwise I would suggest mid-morning, leaving students time beforehand for errands and finishing before lunch appointments.

If you are close to a university or a campus-style workplace, you may find dancers who want to attend during their lunch break. These lessons need to be shorter, allowing time for students to shower and grab a quick bite. Be aware that these students may not have any time flexibility, so keep an eye on the clock as you run these lessons.

If you want to teach children's classes, consider weekday sessions that fit around school hours. If you can teach on a school site, allow just a short break after school for food and bathroom visits. If your students need to travel to reach you, allow for bad traffic. Keep these classes short and upbeat, and consider a price reduction for siblings, nannies, au pairs or babysitting groups.

Most teachers find that their most popular classes are run in the evenings, when people are accustomed to taking recreation and fitness classes. Consider what time the typical working day ends in your area, and whether you want students to come straight from work or to first go home, eat, and change. If you start too early, then your dancers have to rush and arrive stressed. Start too late, and the dancers have become settled at home and don't feel like going out again.

The length of your classes will be a personal choice, but I suggest you start with hour-long classes and lengthen or shorten them, depending on your students:

- Children have a shorter concentration span than adults; you may find it hard to keep their focus beyond forty-five minutes.

- Students attending lunchtime or before-work class may also appreciate a shorter, more intense class.

- Beginners may also prefer to commit to an hour or less. They may be unsure whether they have the fitness for a long class.

Many teachers prefer to run ninety-minute classes, particularly beyond the beginner's level, which gives the class time for technique, drills, choreography, and fun. Although I agree that ninety minutes is the preferred time period to work with intermediate and advanced level students, I break those ninety minutes into two smaller classes of forty-five minutes each, giving the students the opportunity to commit to as much or as little time as they feel ready for.

My aim is always to work toward running convenient classes such as two one-hour classes back to back:

- Beginners
- Level two

An evening can also be broken into three forty-five-minute classes:

- Beginners
- Drills and technique
- Choreography and performance skills

The transition from one class to another should be smooth and easy. For this reason I like to run different levels on the same night and encourage students to attend any or all of the classes. Once beginners have mastered the basic moves, they can work on their technique in a more advanced class, while the advanced dancers can choose where to focus their attention. I always emphasize the idea that belly dancers never grow out of their basic moves and that attending a basic class each week is a core practice for all levels of dancer.

You can encourage dancers to attend more than one class per night by weighting your price in favor of the dancer who books the most. For example, you may price one class at $10, two at $15, and three at $18, if taken on the same night. This also helps to fill up your classes, and full classes are more fun for everyone. If, however, you have limited room in your classes, you may want to set your prices to discourage the more advanced dancers from continuing in your beginner class.

CHOOSING YOUR OWN VENUE

A good venue can make or break your classes, but unfortunately we sometimes have very limited options. Great, cheap, popular rooms may have a waiting list, so you could find yourself limited to a choice of one. Decide if you would prefer to start out self-employed or look for an employer willing to have you teach as a member of staff.

Your search can include dance studios, town halls, church halls, community centers, yoga studios, and gyms. In the UK I did well with community halls, and I found new venues by keeping an eye out for new village halls being built or renovated. They were often worth a few months' wait in return for securing up-to-date facilities. In California I have found it harder to rent space, as so many venues are owned by the city, who would prefer you work for them. Dance studios that focus more on children's classes often have a weekday late evening slot available, or you may find a suitable space in the back room of a coffee shop, restaurant, or bar. Here are some things to consider when looking for a venue:

- Availability
- Cost/rent
- Parking and public transportation
- Cleanliness
- Safety (you may pay more to have a staff member on site)
- Natural light
- Mirrors
- Floor type (sprung floors are wonderful)
- Local population
- Passing foot traffic (this can encourage more students to start or make students feel like they are dancing in a fishbowl)

When looking to rent a venue, ask to see a copy of their contract and take note of how often the rent can be increased, the notice needed to exit the contract, and who is responsible for damage. It is perfectly fine to ask to see their building's insurance and get referrals from others who rent the space so you can get their feedback. It is hard to judge the size of the space you will need, but students seem to be happier to dance in a cramped space with good light and good flooring than a huge, soulless box. Tour the whole building if you can and take a look at the restrooms, changing areas, and any designated parking. If you are going to teach evening classes, go back at night and see how safe it feels. This will be the home for your classes, so take your time to pick a good space. Ask yourself if your students will pay more for a beautiful room in a good neighborhood or be more influenced by price.

Your students will need access, but you may also need to keep strangers out of your hall. It can be very annoying if you have to leave your class to let late arrivers in a main door some distance away. It is even more annoying if the local children use the lobby as a warm, dry place to hang out on cold, wet evenings. Having staff on site is worth the extra cost, although doors secured by keypad entry come a close second.

If you do have trouble from unwanted visitors, I have found that you need to mistake them for belly dancers only once and they soon lose interest. Invite them to join the class, offer them a coin belt, and ask them to pay cash.

APPROACHING EMPLOYERS

You don't have to be your own boss to run a dance class you can be an employee (or a contractor). In this arrangement, most likely you will take either a salary or a percentage of the students' class fees. In return, you avoid having to pay rent, which is your biggest expenditure as a sole proprietor.

Be clear about which parts of the necessary insurance your employer covers and what you are expected to cover yourself. Again, gyms, yoga centers, and dance studios are good places to start looking. A friendly email with a resume and a nice picture attached is a good opening, followed by a personal visit a few days afterward to let them see what kind of person you are. Be prepared to weather a lot of rejection, as many studio owners are hesitant to take a chance on a new class.

Successful dance teachers find studios approaching them all the time, but it is hard to get those first few classes started. County or city councils are more likely to be open to trying a new class, because all it costs them is a listing in their quarterly newsletter. However, it will likely cost you a great deal of form filling and promotion.

No matter which option, getting a first class off the ground will be the biggest hurdle. Once you have one successful class, you can use that as a way to find new venues, tempt new employers, or grow your own classes. All this takes time and perseverance. Don't focus all your efforts in one place, but try and come up with a few new options each week and work hard on presenting yourself as an exciting, effective teacher. This is no different from any other kind of job (or client) hunting.

You may find all your future classes come from your current teaching, as the owners of a gym send someone to check out your class or one of your students opens her own dance studio. Make connections and stay positive: your opportunities will arrive.

When talking money with potential employers, keep in mind both what you want and what they need. Some gyms are going to pay you only the same rate that they pay all their employees, but if that is minimum wage, you may feel they are taking an unfair share of profit from you if you attract thirty students and yet see the equivalent of less than one person's fees in your paycheck.

If you have set up your own business, venue owners may be happier to employ you on a short-term contract or as a guest teacher, in which case you should look for something near a 50/50 split of student fees, but realistically you can expect 35 to 40 percent. Consider where the students are coming from and who is putting the time and effort into contacting them – you or the owner. If they are handing you a full class and have a mailing list of thousands who receive a cute monthly magazine promoting all the classes, then they are going to expect you to take a smaller cut.

PROMOTING YOUR CLASSES

You have your venue, your insurance, your plans, boom box, music – now all you need are some students.

Your first marketing tool will be your website. To begin with, you don't need to spend much money or have any experience in programming to buy a simple template website. (I use Serif WebPlus and Weebly). These do all the programming work for you for little or no payment. I have not found a free website template program with the options to embed video and music, but those are not as essential as getting your class listings onto the Internet.

Go for a domain name that is easy to remember and makes your main business obvious. "RubiesoftheNile.com" or "Sammeraa.com" might say belly dance to you, but a new student might miss it (or misspell it). "www.MyTownBellyDanceClasses.com" is not so poetic, but it sends a clear message about your key business to potential customers. Consider investing in more than one domain name if you feel you may move around, or you want to have a world wide presence, "www.BettiBellyDancer.com" and "www.BettiBellyDancerOfBasingstoke.co.uk". Be aware that sometimes showing an interest in purchasing a domain name may push the price up, so it may be cheaper for you to make an impulse purchase. Make a list of key words before you start looking.

Ask friends for recommendations on good hosting and compare price with availability and reviews. If you are just going to have a template website, you will probably not need to worry so much about support as about cost. The template websites will give you a choice of color and layout options and about five pages to work with. Simplicity can be a virtue: template sites also tend to be clean, well organized, and easy for your customers to use. Start by "storyboarding": divide the information you want to share over a number of sheets of scrap paper and work out what kind of layout you need. Look at other dancers' websites to see how they divide their information and what layouts work for them.

Your color and layout choices will also help your students get to know you. Your website is the first impression you make on potential students, so make it one that attracts the kind of students you want to find. Are you loud, with hot pink and yellow boxes, or do you offer calming shades of gray and blue? Are you a bullet point person or do you write long essays on the history of belly dance? Is your first picture a photo of you, super toned and fit, sweating in front of a mirror at the gym, or are you dancing barefoot on a hillside? Are you laughing with your belly dance gang, or a speck in the distance on a grand stage?

Think about what the potential belly dancers in your town want from a lesson; is that what you are going to provide? If you like to work hard in every lesson and don't stop until everyone is a puddle of sweat, find a picture that highlights your determination. If you like to share the history and culture of the dance, then maybe look for a picture of you in an authentic costume or visiting one of the countries that inspires your dance.

Practical Tip:

As you visit other teachers' websites, ask yourself if you would take their class if you didn't know them, just by judging their opening page and the pictures they provide. Look at the websites of personal trainers. Which of them are going to kick your bottom, and which would be a laugh to work out with? Search the Web for, say, violin teachers: What colors would attract you to pick them as your teacher? How much information would you need to take one of their classes? Look at the websites for salsa teachers: Who looks qualified? Which of them looks like the most fun to dance with?

I suggest you include the following in your website plan:

- Home page, featuring an appealing picture of yourself
- Class schedule, including all booking details
- Page about you: a brief bio and specifics about your belly dance experience
- Frequently Asked Questions (FAQ)
- Terms and conditions
- Testimonials from satisfied students
- Contact information

Other pages will depend on your business. Maybe you need one for your performances, or to help people book you for workshops; maybe you want to link to the restaurant where you dance or show the costumes you make. Keep the side or top navigation bar nice and clear so that people can find their way around easily. People like to look at pretty pictures, but they also want to find the information they need instantly. Read your pages back as if you were totally new to belly dance. Does it answer these questions:

- Where do you teach belly dance?
- When are your classes?
- Do students have to book in advance or can they just turn up?
- Can they come this week?
- How do they book?
- How much will it cost?
- Is there dedicated parking or easy street parking?
- What should they wear?
- How long is the class?
- What will they learn?
- Do they need to bring water?
- Can they call you if they get lost?
- Can they bring their kids?
- Can they try a free class?

I like to include on my website a Frequently Asked Questions page. I find the same problems come up time and time again. Be succinct; don't hide the information in too much text. It doesn't matter how often you say where your classes are, you will always get a phone call or email asking where your venue is and claiming they can't find it on the site. Make it clear and then make it clearer.

Frequently Asked Questions are different from Terms and Conditions. As I see it, the FAQ are just that – practical questions that almost every potential student asks. By answering them on your website, you may reduce the number of times you get asked by prospective students.

Terms and Conditions are considered fine print. Include things people may need to know but that seldom come up in the normal course of a class. You can also consider them the CYA (cover your ass) language, addressing rights, expectations, and rules in the event of a disagreement. Make sure your terms and conditions have their own page and are straightforward and businesslike. They should state, at a minimum, that you can teach whatever you want, however you want, and that students need to pay up front for the privilege of learning from you.

Both your terms and conditions and your FAQ will grow each time someone asks you something unexpected and you realize you need to clarify your rules or add information. Take some time each year to update these; be sure to group similar subjects together.

Everyone wants to have the best website for their area and the highest search engine ratings. Make sure you know how to promote your website by using the page properties and the search functions. These are different with each template, but all are set up to be easy. Search "How to promote my page using X template" and see what suggestions are already online. Use the key words that you imagine your new student will enter into the search engine to find you, and go back regularly to update both your site and the search boxes. Search engines favor websites that are up-to-date and well maintained and have a high click-through rate. Tidying your website and updating it once or twice a month is a good way to keep it fresh and bump it up in the search engine ratings.

Use the search engines to find other marketing opportunities in your area. Enter "[My town] belly dance" and see what listings are highlighted. Your area may have multiple listings pages for dance teachers, evening classes, and activities. It is also worth searching your local competition to see where they are listed. Many listing websites will let you add a photo for free, which is really eye-catching on a page of mostly text listings. Perhaps someone looking for day care may see your beautiful picture under dance teachers and contact you.

I strongly suggest you add your details to www.Shira.net, an "all things belly dance" site that includes a worldwide directory listing many teachers and other resources. Ask Shira if you can link to her website as a great resource for your students. Don't expect to be number one on a search engine, or for Shira to list you the next day, as it takes time to get listed and ranked, but the sooner you start, the sooner you will see your name where it matters.

Review your search engine rankings about once a month and try to find a few more places to add your name and business. Don't be upset if another teacher constantly ranks one or two spots higher than you; instead, see what you can do to make sure new students click on your link instead of hers. If her classes are described as "authentic," maybe change your site so your search results note that yours are "fun." If hers says "Evening classes," make sure yours says "Weekend classes available."

Online social networking has become a great way to connect with your students and to find new ones. It is easier for someone to click a link than to write down your telephone number and remember to pass it on. In addition to your personal, private profile, set up either a profile for yourself as a dancer or a fan page, so that you can focus your postings on dance-related activity and save those about your toddler's finger paintings for your personal profile (although a little of those kinds of posts on your dance page can help students get to know you). Connect with other dancers in your area and search their Friend lists for others you may know to build a good network.

I have had success with advertising on Facebook; although it's not cheap, it can be targeted to focus on the area and age group you are looking to attract. A good Facebook page with a lot of traffic can also appear high on the search engine rankings, so keep it active and upbeat to present an appealing welcome to those exploring the idea of taking a class.

Make sure that all your online activities cross-pollinate each other, linking back to your main website and your key email address. If you promote a class or an event, be sure to include all the booking details, including a link students can use to book online wherever possible. As a quick reality check, try getting from any post, listing, email, or website to a booking site in ten seconds and fewer than four mouse clicks. Then ask a friend to do the same.

I prefer to have a telephone number for my business that is separate from my personal cell phone number. I have had a number of nuisance calls over the years, so I don't often answer the phone to numbers I don't know (Caller ID is a must). Obviously, if you are a dancer looking for gigs you must be prepared to answer calls if that is where your work is going to come from. I would rather deal with people via email, and I am lucky that I can do that. Invest in a "number for life" that links to your cell phone but can be moved from one mobile device to another as you change phones or areas. This means that you can print up business cards or post on websites and be pretty sure you will still have the same number in five years. Some "number for life" websites also give you a list of numbers to choose from, so you can pick the area code where you work if it's different from where you live. You might also go for a catchy or memorable "phoneword" phone number (spelled out by the related letters on the phone numeric pad).

It's a good idea to have some postcard-sized flyers with you at all times, along with a few push-pins, so you can leave them on bulletin boards in coffee shops or supermarkets. Some places post rules about what you can or cannot post. I leave a space on my postcards for a small logo, as my local library won't take flyers without the city logo printed on them. Before you order thousands of flyers or cards, it is worth checking these things. Include the essentials: what (belly dance classes!), where, when, how much, who with, and how to sign up.

I have found my best supply of new students has always come from recommendations by those attending class. Do ask your students to take a flyer for a friend or post a recommendation on their social network page. They understand that you want to build your business, and they are already invested in your success. Make them an offer they can't refuse – like one free class if they bring a friend.

Beware of those offering you the chance to attract more students by dancing or teaching for free. In my experience these offers never work out in your favor, and I've felt like a fool for being too trusting. If a gathering stands to benefit from having you dance or teach, then they will find a way to pay you, even if you feel like offering a reduced price. The promise of future students rarely turns into reality.

That is not to say you can't give away your skills wherever you want, but always think of it in monetary terms, and don't offer your skills for free if that also stops a fellow teacher from being paid. Each year I give up a morning in December to teach children in a local school for no fee; I also offer one morning each June at a different school where I do charge. The first school cannot afford to pay outside teachers, and I strongly believe in the work they do for their kids. The other school can afford me. My December morning is a gift from me to a very special group of children, but giving one organization a gift does not mean that I have to gift my time or skills to everyone.

In the UK I also danced at my local village fete each year. It was my way of supporting an event that built our community and helped local charities. Some years I was invited to dance at a different fete every weekend of the summer. That involved rushing home from teaching class, showering, changing, packing, putting on makeup, filling up the gas tank, burning a CD, and giving up an afternoon with my children. For those events, I charged. Each of them would let me hand out flyers to the crowd, but it was unlikely that I would find new students at each fete. Of course, for each flyer you hand out there is a chance that someone might come, or they might tell a friend, but you have to hand out a lot of flyers to fill a class. Your time and skills are valuable; give them as gifts only when you really want to.

Finally, whether you are handing out flyers or building a website, calling venues or putting photos up on social network sites, because it's all about belly dance, you are likely to get some negative reaction. How you handle that will be up to you, but I feel it's only fair to warn you. I have always had wonderful support for my job from all my family, but we can't pretend that society as a whole doesn't have some weird ideas about what it is we do. I have handed out flyers that have been handed straight back with a look of disgust. I have had venues refuse to let me rent because their image of belly dance doesn't fit in with their mission statement. And, sadly, I have had abusive phone calls and online troll encounters. By becoming a belly dance teacher you are moving away from a private hobby and into the public eye. As with everything else in life, you will find there are some people you can educate and others you can't. I don't like to look for trouble; my pictures are modest, I don't use "Exotic" or "Sexy" on my flyers, but trouble still finds me. Remember that you know more about this dance than they do; you know how it makes you feel, and how wonderful it can be to dance, and that is why you want to share the dance with others. Their ideas about belly dance are just that: their ideas. They don't change who you are or what you do.

I hope that things will get better as belly dance becomes more mainstream and we bring quality dancing to more venues. Never take their comments personally; over time, you will learn when it is better to walk away than to stay and argue.

PACKING YOUR BAGS

As a belly dance teacher or performer, you'll have a lot to carry around with you. You'll want to invest in a good, strong, big bag. You don't want to be crushing your kit, so pick something that will comfortably hold everything you could need, plus a dozen veils. If you will be using public transportation or have a lot of stairs to climb, you may prefer a daypack; otherwise I strongly suggest you get a case on wheels to minimize the amount of lifting and carrying you have to do. Belly dance teachers need to take good care of their bodies, and lifting a heavy bag in and out of a car ten times a week will not help your back.

Pack a very basic first aid kit. Depending on what kind of first aid training you have, you may want to pick out a prepackaged kit or assemble one yourself, but it is useful to have it in a red bag prominently labeled "first aid kit" in case someone else needs to go through your bag and find the right treatment. I like the kind of ice pack you activate by breaking the seal; also include some adhesive bandages, compression wraps, and sterile solution. I hope you will only have to deal with a few blisters. If you have an injury in your class, always ask whether anyone else there is more qualified than you to treat the patient, and make it clear that you are offering first aid as a friend, not an expert. If in doubt, always call for help.

Unless your studio provides a sound system, you will need to get some kind of speakers or CD player. I suggest you look for something in the 30-watt range. The average set of home speakers will just be too quiet to fill a large room, so look for something that is marketed to be suitable for outdoor or large room sound. Beyond volume, you probably don't need any other features, unless you like to increase the bass. It is useful to have both a power cord and batteries in case the power goes out at your venue. Some teachers like to have a remote control, but I find it bothersome to dance with; also, returning to the speakers gives me the chance for a sip of water and to check my lesson plan. If you intend to run parties or hafla, look into buying or borrowing a professional sound system or speakers from musicians. A guitar amp will plug into most sound systems and create a lot more sound, taking your powerful speakers up to mini concert level.

Decide how you are going to present your music. Some teachers still prefer CDs, but most have moved on to the iPod or other personal music player. The iPod has the advantage of allowing you to prepare your music plan in advance and have it all ready to run before you arrive in class. Be sure to pack a charger in your bag.

If you have access to a CD player in your studio, it can be useful to prepare a backup CD for your bag with a couple of warm-up tracks, something with a regular beat, something more suitable to a soft move, a shimmy track, and a few tracks you can imagine writing a group choreography to someday. If your phone is capable, it's a good idea to prepare a similar playlist to keep on there. This enables you to teach a lesson even if your iPod locks up or runs down. You can still teach the moves you wanted to, then ask your students to come up with a combination or a choreography, no matter what level you are working with.

Finally, just to be sure you will never be without music, it is helpful to pack a set of finger cymbals; even if you are not a confident player, most of us can maintain a good regular beat to teach along to.

I'll cover how to prepare lesson plans shortly; for now, know that you will want some way of keeping your lesson plans neat. I like a clear, multipage folder, so I can see the lesson and also check back on previous lessons if need be. It is useful to also include your term plan so you can answer student questions about later lessons or double check whether you covered a move earlier in the term.

If you will be taking money in class, you should have cash on hand so you can give change. The cash you need will depend on your pricing. If your class price is $20 and your currency includes $20 bills and $10 bills, then you might assume that most people will pay with a $20, but it is worth having some extra $10s in case someone brings a $50. If, however, you charge $17, you will need lots of $1s to give everyone $3 change for their $20. I suggest you start off with a cash reserve approximately twice that of a single lesson fee and in small denominations. It won't take you long to figure out what kind of bills your students tend to bring.

In large classes it can be useful to set up a desk just outside the door with a cash box and register so that people can pay on their way in. The problem is, you may need a helper to run your front desk, as students will be arriving right up until the start time, giving you little time to set up your teaching station. I've found a wonderful solution: I offer a discount price to a young student or someone who wants more classes than they can afford, in return for running the front desk for me. Just be aware that you may not be able to offer this at every venue or long term. Perhaps ask for help the first week of a new block of lessons or in January when those New Year resolutions to get fit kick in. The alternative is an honesty box where students pay, register, and help themselves to change. I have had good experiences with an honesty box, but it may take you some time to trust your students to that level. For my honesty box I use a large, bright purse with a wide neck. I set it wide open so students don't have to dig too deep to find their change. It is quick and easy to close, and the bright color means everyone in class will notice if it goes missing. Set it up along with the register a little distance from where the students store their bags, so no one can interfere with it while appearing to look in their own bag.

Even if you don't know who will be coming to class, it is useful to set up a class register ahead of time. This can simply be a sheet with a printed grid, with one column of longer boxes where students can fill in their names and columns for the class dates where they can check their attendance. I also ask students to add their email address, even though I also ask for this on their waiver. Sometimes it is useful to see it written out again if you need to check spelling. If you are teaching through adult education, the administrators may provide a register. Always take an extra minute or two for a head count and check that against your register; should you ever be involved in a fire, earthquake, or other emergency evacuation, you will be expected to know how many people were in your room at the start of your lesson.

Finally, depending on your lesson you may need a bag of finger cymbals, veils, or props to lend to students. It is good to start building a collection of these as soon as possible. Sticks are easier to carry in mass in some plastic tubing, like gutter piping, or wrapped with hair bands. Cheap dance sticks may be tempting, but I've found they can be too light to hold up to a ten-week course. I prefer a more folkloric stick, which I purchase from seaside gift shops. Start your collection of cheap veils by visiting charity and thrift shops looking for fabric or sarongs; for finger cymbals, approach belly dance traders to ask about bulk buying.

Here is a quick checklist for organizing your bag:

- CDs/iPod
- Player/speakers
- Cables/chargers/batteries
- Lesson plans
- Handouts
- First aid kit
- Finger cymbals/zills
- Backup CD/playlist on your phone
- Pens/note paper
- Business cards
- Cash box
- Class list/register
- Water/coin belt/dance shoes for you
- Perfume/deodorant/wet wipes
- Hair clips
- Keys/pass codes for entry into venue

I bring a file folder with a few handouts for my students and business cards they can help themselves to in case they want to pass my details on to a friend. I also include flyers for local events, handouts with music suggestions, and a list of my upcoming performances. It is good for your students to know you are a busy belly dancer and part of a wider community.

HANDOUTS

Handouts might seem old-fashioned in teaching today, when so much can be shared over the Internet, but being able to put a piece of paper into a student's hand instantly boosts the odds of your information being read and understood. Handouts enable you to start a discussion, answer questions, and give dance or music examples in class time. A well-written handout can also reduce misunderstandings between you and your students. You will find complete handout examples later in the book; for now, I'll mention a few handouts I like to share with my classes:

A welcome letter - This includes my details, the goals of the class, and some housekeeping matters. I ask them to arrive on time, to bring water, and to use the lockers provided. I tell them about my dance experience, what I hope they will get out of the class, and their path into the more advanced classes.

A waiver form - Students sign this to absolve you from any liability should they be injured or have anything stolen. I like to list health conditions that may hinder their dancing. It's amazing how many people forget they have an old back injury until prompted. I include a declaration that they feel fit and healthy enough to take part in a dance class. I also list other things that may happen that I cannot be responsible for. Here are a few things you may want to list:

- Students will take care of their own body, welfare, and belongings.
- Students will not hold the teacher responsible for any loss or injury while at the venue, practicing, performing, or partying.
- Students need to make sure that they arrive for the warm up during class and warm up before practice sessions at home.
- Students will take note of all warnings.
- Students should aim to maintain good posture at all times.
- Students are asked to allow their teacher to use touch as a teaching method while others are present in the room.

You may want to add more to this list. This waiver is unlikely to protect you if you do something willfully hurtful or stupid with your students, but it is important to point out to them that every activity can be potentially harmful and to highlight the most likely ways they could injure themselves. Once you have the waiver forms signed, retain them somewhere safe. Sometimes dancers like to take home their own copy, so provide duplicate forms.

Make sure that it is clear that all students must sign a waiver before attending your class. If you should ever lose an important waiver form, or if the person who hurts herself is the one and only one who never signed, then I hope you have a class full of people willing to say you always ask for a signed waiver. I recommend consulting a lawyer for advice about wording to include in your waiver.

> **A contact form** - This is a request for details I can add to my mailing list. I like to collect email addresses, as that is my preferred method for sending out special offers and news updates. It is also useful in case your venue ever closes and you have to inform your students within a few hours of their lesson.

I think that three handouts at a first lesson is plenty, but again, I also like to give them my business card, so they have my contact details in their purse or posted on their fridge.

Over the weeks of class, I may give them more handouts on topics like the history of dance, styles of belly dance, and of course choreography. It is nice when working on one piece of music to also give them some details on the artist, the music style, and the lyrics.

When preparing for a performance, I have lots of extra handouts – I've got examples of those later in the book.

On all your handouts, include your name, website, telephone number, and a copyright notice. You may also want to add a picture or logo or print them on colored paper. This reduces the chance of your handouts being lost in the student's purse or on their paperwork pile at home. Print out enough handouts for everyone to have two, and bring them week after week.

WHAT TO WEAR

At this point you may be happy to wear the same kind of clothes as you wear to attend classes, and that is fine, but I suggest putting a little more thought into how you dress and style yourself as a teacher. Think about brighter colors, top of the range skirts or yoga pants, fitted t-shirts or wrap tops and a signature look like a flower in your hair or an exceptional bracelet collection.

I once arrived early to teach a workshop and set up my table, handouts, and sound system before going back to my bag to get a drink. An attendee joined me, and we started chatting about the other workshops she had been to that day. Out of the blue, she said, "I hear this teacher is a really big lady, so I'm not sure how she is going to teach us fitness drills." There was nothing I could do but pause for a moment, introduce myself, and make light of her comment. I realized that I had dressed for a workout, but my look was so basic that she had assumed I was a fellow student.

As the teacher of a belly dance class, you have to stand out and be exceptional. How you do that will depend on your own style and the persona you want to project, but take time now to make a decision. If you wear yoga pants, your students will wear yoga pants. If you wear makeup, your students will wear makeup. If you wear all black, your students will lean toward the dark side. Your clothes need to be functional but also reflect your professionalism. Here are a few common mistakes you can avoid:

Don't wear overly long or wide pants. You will either stand on them and slip or bruise your feet or spend the whole lesson tucking them in or tying them up or rolling up the cuffs. Buy pants that are a little shorter.

Don't forget your layers. If you teach in a full skirt, you will spend half of your time with it tucked into your waist or lifted to show your feet. Make sure you have on cycle shorts, harem pants, or leggings underneath. Underwear is essential.

Don't wear too much jewelry. While it's nice to show off some beautiful pieces you own, you may also find yourself accidentally throwing them at your students as you spin, turn, or lift your arms. A bangle to the forehead will make for an interesting visit to the emergency room.

Don't dress too busy. I love yoga pants with multicolored stripes as much as the next person, but if your students have to spend an hour watching them bouncing at the front of the room, they may leave with a migraine.

Don't try to be invisible. Some of us are lucky enough to have mirrored studios, but sometimes you find yourself dancing in a very black place. Wear a black skirt and T-shirt in front of a black wall, and your students will be as lost as you are.

Don't wreck your best costumes. It's tempting to think of class as a whole new audience for your beautiful costumes, but you should expect to sweat just as much as your students. Nothing eats sequins as quickly as perspiration, and nothing will bankrupt a dancer as quickly as needing a new wardrobe every few months.

Don't tie your coin belt to one side. I know everyone else does, but from the student's point of view it looks like you are dancing lopsided. Tie it in the middle or wear something more even, like a tube mini skirt, over your skirt or pants. Unless you do dance lopsided, in which case I suggest some hard drills!

Don't overwhelm them with fragrance. As a belly dancer you are allowed to smell a touch exotic, but many people are very sensitive to scents; some are even allergic. A quick spritz of an off-the-shelf perfume before you leave the house will be fine, but there is no need to perfume the room, your veils, or the whole street. As dancers we are right to be worried that our costume may smell of old restaurants or body odor, but keeping up-to-date with the laundry will take care of that. Also, it's best to avoid smelling of marijuana, as that may not appeal to your customers, and perfume doesn't do a very good job of disguising that particular smell.

Control your hair. Many of us have invested our time and special products into growing beautiful, long "belly dancer" hair, but it can be a huge distraction in class. Keep it away from your face and tie or pin it up.

Shoes or bare feet? This is a personal preference, but either way, keep your feet clean and safe. Even the top dance teachers have to sweep the floor and pack baby wipes to clean their soles.

Body hair is a personal thing, but you may want to switch to an "invisible" deodorant rather than use one that coats your underarms with white powder.

PLANNING 101

Lesson planning is the most important part of preparing for your classes; it often takes twice as long as the actual lessons. It is useful to have an idea of the students you are expecting, but also to be adaptable and think about how your plan will change depending on your attendees. Before you meet your students, think about what their goals may be, how often/long you will meet with them, and over what time line. Do you want to take them from beginner to performer in ten weeks, a year, or five years? Can you offer them the potential for weight loss, or would you rather they learn to free dance to your drum playing? Do you want them to appear in your end-of-term showcase? Or would you like them to be able to enjoy all the different styles of belly dance as audience members?

Try mixing your goals with those of the students and selecting a list of around four for each set of classes. Your goals do not have to be measurable, but they should be achievable within the allotted time frame. Here are some ideas for course goals:

- To gain good posture
- To be able to demonstrate the top ten basic moves
- To be able to perform a choreography
- To be able to free dance to a simple tune
- To know the top ten styles of belly dance
- To know the most commonly used instruments in belly dance music
- To know the film stars of the golden age of belly dance
- To be able to follow a lead in group improvisation
- To have fun
- To be able to dance a veil entrance
- To be able to play five drum patterns on the finger cymbals
- To be confident when dancing with a stick
- To be able to write a choreography
- To be able to show a shaabi feel in your dancing
- To understand the base dances from which we fuse
- To improve fitness

From your long-term goals and your short list of current goals, you will be able to group your lessons into eight-, ten-, or twelve-week terms or semesters.

If you are teaching through an adult education system, your term length may be set for you, but even if you work for yourself it is useful to plan in chunks that fit into the seasons or between holidays. Once you know your students, you can always ask them what their goals are—either verbally or with another handout they return to you—and use those to guide your planning.

Before focusing on moves or choreography, it's a good idea to work out a set of objectives for your session of classes; you may want to consider:

- How to form an interesting and informative course
- How to set the level for your students, to be interesting and challenging but not so complex as to be off-putting
- How to prepare the dancers for more advanced lessons
- How to nurture and retain loyal customers
- How to cover the basic moves, posture, shimmies, and also some history, performance skills, music options, styles, artists
- How to prepare the dancers for any events you would like them to attend out in the wider belly dance community, be that as a performer or as an educated audience member

These objectives set the tone of the lessons rather than the content. Here are the objectives of my current beginners class:

- To foster confidence in and love of free dance
- To use upbeat music from around the world
- To encourage reenrollment in future courses
- To encourage attendance at local performances
- To keep everyone safe and happy
- To focus on posture in all exercises

SEMESTER/TERM PLANNING – BEGINNERS

Any extra time or energy you can put into semester planning will pay off in the long run. You may find yourself short of time in the coming months, so take time to prepare now. Don't set your term plan in stone, but also keep referring back to it each week. If you are teaching multiple classes, it can be easy to miss an important move or duplicate exercises. Good preparation makes you look professional and does wonders for your mental state.

The first challenge is what to teach and what to leave until next time. In our enthusiasm, it is easy to try and throw all the amazing topics at our students too quickly, which not only overpowers the students but also leaves us with nothing to teach them in the future. Decide how long your term or semester is going to be and then set about writing some lists.

Your first list should be of everything you think students need to have covered before leaving beginners and moving into an intermediate class. You may feel you want to move students upward quickly, in which case your list should be shorter than if you want them to stay in beginners for a year. Personally, I find it better to try and keep students at the beginner level for twenty to thirty weeks. Less, and they feel out of their depth in the next level class; more, and they are constantly going over the same material and become bored. I don't think that I can cover everything they need to know any quicker, but I also know that they won't get into any subject in depth until I can teach them in an intermediate class without the distraction of beginner moves.

List one: Everything beginner level, or the big List

When writing your "everything beginners need to know" list, don't forget the layers. Do your intermediate students need to be able to do a hip rotation, and large and small rotations, pivoting and undulating (with rise and fall) and travelling and shimmying rotations? Do they have to be able to hold a frame while rotating, or do you want a set arm movement? Do you need to see that rotation on demand or used in free dance? Now, looking at just one move, you have already made a long list:

- Hip rotation
- Small hip rotation
- Large hip rotation
- Pivoting rotation
- Undulating rotation
- Travelling rotation

- Framed rotation
- Swing door arms with rotation
- Falling leaf hands with rotation
- Shimmy over a rotation
- Use a rotation in free dance

Of course, you may add to this list depending on your style of dance. You might like to see a rotation travelling to the side, or a corkscrewed rotation, or a rotation with a veil. You might like a broken rotation where the dancer bounces on her heels, or an umi. With just one move we have already found sixteen things we want to teach! And if we assume each will take ten minutes, that is more than two and a half hours of teaching. Add in time for warm-ups and cooldowns, and rotations could fill the first four lessons. It would be very boring for the students. So once you have your huge list, it's time to sort out what is really important, what is fun, and what is going to have to wait a while.

Practical Tip:

Continuing with rotations on the hips, think about any moves or layers that are not included on my list. Now decide at what point in their dancing careers you want your students to learn these. Are they needed from the first few classes, or within the first ten weeks? The first six months, or the first year? What moves can you save to teach in a more advanced course?

The big list takes all the belly dance moves and multiplies them by every variation in the way we dance them. Almost every move can be done while walking, turning, undulating, shimmying, with framed arms or flowing, with soft knees or a bounce, clockwise and counterclockwise, upward, downward, and to either side.

Practical Tip:

Write a list of every move you know and every way you know to dance it. This will be a huge list. You may want to use my hip rotation example as a starting point. When you have finished this list, leave it for a week and then come back to add to it. You may find you come back to it every few months.

List two: Only the essentials or key moves

This is an important list, because your big list is way too much to teach to beginners in just ten or even twenty hours of lessons. Now you have to decide what you are going to teach if these next ten weeks are the only time you will ever spend with a student. You really want to keep this list as short as possible. Here is my list:

- American style belly dance - An introduction
- Arm frames
- Camel
- Fashion in belly dance wear
- Figure eight
- Forward and back step
- Hip drop
- Hip lift
- Hip rotations
- Introduction to free dance
- Introduction to veil
- Maya /outward eight
- Popular music choices
- Posture
- Reverse figure eight
- Shimmy
- Shoulder shimmies
- Side to side push
- Snake arms
- Three-quarter walk/shimmy
- Travelling shimmy
- Walking, belly dance style

From time to time my list changes, but the core moves stay the same. I think that being able to free dance is important; you may disagree, but we probably all agree that hip drops need to be on that list.

Teaching only from this list would be very limiting. It is limiting for you to teach, limiting to learn, and doesn't really prepare the student for the next level. This is why we needed that first big list and why we are now going to divide it up, distribute its contents, and spice up each beginners term with a sprinkling of the more exciting stuff.

Whether you work in terms or semesters or continue through the year, it's a good idea to divide your planning into manageable sets. For this example, I am going to divide my year by the seasons – spring, summer, fall, and winter – as I tend to teach semesters that roughly work into that pattern each year.

I divide all those extra moves or concepts from the big list into four lists. I am looking for balance here. I don't want one list to be all about hip drops , but I also don't want it to be all about pivoting. So pivoting hip drops go in the fall list, pivoting lift goes in spring, pivoting figure eight is in summer, and pivoting rotations go in the winter list. Now that I have pivoting rotations in the winter list, I need to split the other rotation moves into other lists, so hip rotations with snake arms get covered in spring, travelling rotations go on the summer list, and undulating rotations are added to fall.

You may find that scraps of paper you can shuffle around are a good way to set up these lists. My lists also include some history topics, performance skills, and choreographing.

When I looked at my lists this year, it was obvious that in spring I should mostly focus on history and styles of dance, summer contained everything I needed to teach veil, and fall gave me the opportunity to introduce the different instruments and some free dance concepts. Finally, I like to finish the year with a term that is mostly focused on choreography, but I try to write it at the beginning of the year so that I know which moves to focus on.

This gives each of my terms a slightly different feel and tone. You may come up with a few different ideas for the overall feel of each of your terms and need to shuffle some of the moves around to fit. If you want to move your students up quickly, you will need to select less and not teach in too much depth. If you want them to stay in beginners for a long time, you need to make each term new and fresh in some way to keep them coming back for more.

I think you are looking for between fifteen and twenty additional moves or concepts from the big list in each "season" list for a ten-week course – just enough to give each class a couple of more interesting things to do in their lesson, but not so many that you have to rush through them.

Now that you have two lists of concepts and ideas, you can pull strategically from the big list to enhance your essentials and form a semester plan. The first thing you need to do is work out how many weeks you will be teaching and whether there are any breaks or special events to prepare for. Perhaps your employer wants your dancers to perform at an open day, or you have a long holiday break in the middle, or you want to keep the last lesson for learning choreography or for playing some party games.

In the following example, I am planning a ten-week course, but I have taught everything from four weeks to twenty. Regardless of class length, the theory stays the same.

Start with a big piece of scrap paper and begin penciling in some activities. I like to start at week one, when I know we need to allocate ten minutes to paperwork, finding the room, introducing ourselves, and talking about belly dance in general. Next I will spend longer than usual working on posture, perhaps making some corrections. Then we have our warm-up, and I like to do something lighthearted, maybe a game, or have them clap along to a drum or learn some belly dance style walks. The idea of this first exercise is to break the ice, to make them feel happy and at home. Toward the end of the class I like to break down the shimmy, and I always end with a cooldown. Assuming a one-hour class and allocating all of those ten minutes each, that hour is full.

The problem is that those activities might fill the hour, or I might be done within the first half hour, so I am going to add two more moves. I am going to pick two simple moves that everyone should be able to do. I suggest hip rotations, lifts or drops, figure eights or side to sides. You may have another move you think is more suitable. I will pick something soft and something sharp. That not only provides interest and contrast but also helps you to assess the class and students' strengths and weaknesses and gives you something to add to for the next week. Although I am putting those two moves on the term plan, I will not be upset if they don't get done until the next week.

As we are accepting that class time in week one may be swallowed up in the process of completing paperwork and welcoming, week two needs to include those two moves and maybe a couple more. Don't forget to again cover posture and paperwork in case some new faces turn up. Perhaps it's OK to add a layer to one of last week's moves.

By week three you are looking to close the gaps. Have all your moves so far been on the hips? Have you been stationary? Do they know what to do with their arms? Consider adding a couple of moves to fill those gaps. Again, we are looking at planning four or five activities but only needing to cover three.

For week four I may be guided by the overall topic, such as history or instruments or choreography. If I want to talk about American Tribal Style (ATS), the lesson would include single hip lifts, or I might want to do snake arms to a violin to tie into a study of the instruments. As you move through the weeks, you will see that some moves or concepts need to wait until others before they can be done. For example, the three-quarter shimmy or Egyptian walk can be done only by dancers who are confident with their lifts and drops. If you wait too long before teaching those, then the term will run out on you. Some moves, like the camel (sometimes called an undulation or body roll), are hard to do if you are not used to using particular muscles and so are best left until mid-term when the dancer has become used to using her core. Personally I find free dance easier to introduce early so that the dancers have only three or four moves to choose from; otherwise they ask you "Now, what moves do I know again?" and you break the flow of the lesson.

Toward the mid-term you may feel your lessons are becoming just a list of moves, so it is a good idea to add in something more exciting or challenging at this stage. By allocating the moves to different weeks, some ideas will jump out at you. If all your moves are soft, perhaps you would like to talk about a taqsim or introduce the veil. If everything is beat driven, you may want to try letting them free dance to something folkloric.

As your plan moves toward the end of the term, think about getting your students motivated to sign up for the next session. Can you plan some games for the last week or a big review so they can feel proud of all they have learned? They may be ready to be split up into groups to write their own choreography, or you could set up tables and chairs in the style of a restaurant and let them dance in that space.

Finally, it is time to put your term plan onto one or two sheets of paper, making it easier for you to refer back to. I like to give myself a set of objectives at the top to keep me focused on what is really important about the semester. It is useful to keep all the dates and lesson num-

bers so that you know where you are in your term.Some teachers keep a notes column so that they can mark down any problems they had with the lesson. You might find it helpful to note student numbers if your center doesn't give you a register, or just list any student absences so that you can take some time later in the course to revisit the moves those dancers missed.

TERM PLANNING – MORE ADVANCED CLASSES

When setting up your term planning for more advanced lessons, you can start again with your main objectives as a guide. Perhaps you would like your students to be ready to perform choreography for the summer show, or you want them to be confident in improvising with their zills. Maybe you want to spend some weeks developing their folkloric dance style or dancing to classic hits or improving their arms or fitness. Whatever you fancy, you just need to start with one good idea. Turn that good idea into smaller parts and build those into interesting lessons.

I cover teaching choreography in a later chapter, but initially I would look at the choreography and break it into small chunks. I would set aside the last two or three weeks as polishing time, letting the dancers run through the choreography fully and giving feedback on the small details such as arm placements and smiles. I would start with the part that they need to be most confident in and break down combinations for them to drill. I build in lots of time for skills that will help them understand the music, strengthen weaknesses, and isolate moves.

Here is a rough sketch for a choreography term:

Week one:
Break down moves for combo one
Work on arm strength and drills
Free dance to music
Discuss history, lyrics, and mood of music

Week two:
Break down moves for combo two
Go back over moves for combo one
Teach combo one
Demo combo one and two to music

Week three:
Break down moves for combo three
Go back over combo one
Introduce combo two
Put combos one and two together

Week four:
Drill combo two
Introduce combo three
Break down opening moves
Run through opening to end of combo three

Week five:
Drill combo three
Focus on opening, mood, group dynamics, staging
Run through opening until end of combo three

Week six:
Drill problem areas
Set up the ending
Discuss ending and taking applause
Run through the whole thing

Week seven:
Run the whole choreography
Work on problem areas
Talk about suitable costume and makeup

Week eight:
Run the whole choreography
Discuss performance skills
Fine tune move size, face positions, arms
Split up the group so each can watch
Ask how history, lyrics, mood show in
　choreography
Ask students to prepare for dress rehearsal
　next week

Week nine:
Run the whole choreography
Ask for weak spots and problems
Check costumes, makeup
Praise the group

Week ten:
Run the whole choreography
Allocate a combo to each group to play with,
　perhaps by adding a prop or zills or to set
　up a different performance setting or as a
　duet/trio
Ask for feedback

Obviously, your term plan is going to depend on how difficult your choreography is and how well prepared your students are. You may need to split it into fifteen combinations and spend a ten-week course working on those, or you may be able to teach the whole thing in one ninety-minute session. The aim of a choreography term should be not just to learn a dance, but also to learn new moves or ways to use those moves in interesting ways.

Let us imagine you would like to teach a term on dancing with a veil. Veil dancing is very popular and a skill that every belly dancer needs to master. It is a good term to teach early on, and I would combine it with revisiting some basic moves to make sure my dancers have a strong foundation and can also dance with the veil rather than dance, stop and do some veil work, dance . . . You may want to teach choreography as part of this term or to save that as something to do the next term, once they have the skills.

Here is a rough sketch for a veil term:

Week one:
Interesting belly dance walks
Choosing your veil
Making an entrance with your veil
Swapping veils to see what you like
Holds
Drills to strengthen arms
Walking with a veil

Week two:
Framing yourself with a veil
Frames with key moves
Partner work, picking out a favorite move and picking a frame to match
Partner or small group work, moving from one move to the next with interesting frames

Week three:
Twirling the veil
Twirling with rotations, figure eights, camels
Group work – frame to twirl to frame – writing their own combo

Week four:
Basic turns
Turning and twirling
Travelling with a frame into travelling with a twirl – cross the floor work

Week five:
Turning with frames
Flicks
Overhead throws
Envelope
All of the above, layered over favorite move
Small group work, building combinations where the veil is the star

Week six:
Kisses and pyramid turns
Tucking and untucking during turns
Teacher's signature or favorite veil moves
Travelling with signature moves

Week seven:
Choreography without the veil

Week eight:
Choreography with the veil

Week nine:
Revisit favorite moves
Group work on combinations
Choreography

Week ten:
Double veil (dancing with two veils at once)
Duets – working with passing the veil between partners without breaking the flow of the dance
Choreography
Games with veils

This kind of planning works with any style that you would like to teach. Take your time picking a subject and perhaps spend a year or so preparing. If you would like to teach something like khaleggi, the idea usually comes from a workshop or an inspiring performance. Pencil it into your diary as a topic for a year from now and consider taking three or four workshops with different teachers in preparation. Purchase a video or two and start practicing. It is inspiring for your students to see you dance, so work on a number for yourself in that style. You will need a collection of music in the right style to prepare to fill ten hours or more, so make some purchases.

You will find that the preparation times overlap, so you may be working on improving your own shaabi, veil, and khaleggi dance all at the same time. Keep notes, and record yourself dancing. Ideally, by the end of the year you will have more than enough information to fill the term. Of course, sometimes it's nice to be more spontaneous and take something that inspires you to your class that same day. I think that it's fine to inject your enthusiasm in that way, but it's not good for long-term teaching. The students get random information and not enough contexts. Better to tease them with ideas that you are working on for their next term (which also encourages reenrollment) and deliver their course fully formed once it is perfect.

LESSON PLANNING

Lesson planning is all about taking your term plan and making it fit the time you have available to teach each lesson. Keep each lesson interesting but also follow a set form, so that the students have a mix of new ideas and the comfort of familiarity. The hardest thing about lesson planning is time management, and that is something that you will master only by teaching and planning and teaching some more.

I like to divide my time into five-minute segments, although some teachers prefer ten-minute segments. Go with whatever suits you best. Assuming that I am teaching an hour, my basic format looks like this:

The first five minutes of class is the meet and greet; take money, fill forms, organize room, and discuss posture. This may be different for you if you have students who arrive early or an admin area at your venue where administrative things can happen, but in my classes I find the first five minutes always disappears, and if I plan an activity for those first five minutes, I start each lesson behind schedule. During the meet-and-greet it's a nice idea to check whether everyone is feeling well and has had a good week. Take a moment to say a few words about today's class and how it relates to previous lessons and the course as a whole:

> *"Hello. How is everyone? Thanks for coming out tonight. So last week we worked really hard on some soft moves, and I would like to take some time today to focus on beautiful arms to match. I have a new move for you that I think you are going to love. Then after our shimmy we are going to dance to a pretty little love song that I have picked out for you. Oh, and don't forget, if you wanted to see the belly dance show, it is this Saturday; flyers about how to get your tickets are on the desk. If everyone is ready? Posture . . ."*

After the meet and greet, my average class time continues with:

0:05 – Soft warm-up
More details on this on page 91.

0:10 – Heart rate warm-up
This is where we up the tempo and raise the heart rate. More details on page 91.

0:15 – Repeat of last week's work; introduce this week's work
This may be time spent on a move we did last week, or a subject I asked them to look at for homework. I may cover history or context in this segment or explain to them the point of the work we are going to do. I may explain how a combination is going to help us with choreography or how a drill will tone the gluteus muscles.

0:20 – Cover content of the term plan
This may be a couple of moves, some combos, or group work. I look at the list I developed in my term planning, and we work our way through everything that has been allocated to this week.

0:45 – Shimmy practice
I like to shimmy in every class. Students seem to need regular focus on their shimmies to help build them over time. You might like to mix them up into improvised drum solos or make them into an intense drill. Sometimes a class will enjoy focusing on one shimmy combination for a few weeks in a row or a particular shimmy skill, such as thigh shimmies or shifting weight.

0:50 – Ta-dah!
I like to end each lesson with a reason why we did the work we covered, which I call the Ta-dah! moment. It might be as simple as giving them the chance to dance along while watching my bum as I make the three moves we just learned fill a short piece of music. Sometimes it will be the coming together of the point I made earlier. I may have them split up into two groups so they can see how cool the combo looks, or travel the floor using a new style. This part of the lesson should be the thing they remember when someone asks them what they did in class that day; it makes up for any dull drills or endless repitions earlier in the class. More details on the Ta-Dah moment on page 102.

0:55 – Cooldown
This is a time to bring the heart rate down. Examples on page 106.

In summary, most lessons will look a little like this:

0:00 – Meet and greet
0:05 – Soft warm-up
0:10 – Heart rate warm-up
0:15 – Revisit or introduce topic
0:20 – Term plan content
0:45 – Shimmy
0:50 – Ta-dah!
0:55 – Cooldown

You can see that although this lesson involves teaching for an hour, the content that you have worked on for your term plan has to fill only twenty-five minutes or so each week.

I would break that down into five-minute sections and allocate an activity to each section. Don't try and teach a new move every five minutes. Teaching each move will take longer than that. But you won't necessarily need five minutes to break down and explain the move and then five minutes to put it into the muscle memory with practice or drills. The twenty-five minutes gives us time for two or three ideas or moves. Prioritize these so that you can plan three but you have to cover only two if the time gets away from you.

Perhaps your term plan says "hip rotations, hip drops, and walks." For me, the first two are more important, and the walks are something that can be bumped or moved to later in the term. If we don't do the hip drops and rotations, that might hold back activities planned for later in the term. However, if your choreography starts with an interesting walk onto the stage, then that might be a priority for your planning and should be covered in that class.

You may find that the students are great at hip rotations and cover that in just five minutes, but the hip drops are not working, with half the class trying to lift and lots of bouncy knees. You should still only give it ten minutes, otherwise the dancers will get bored, so make a note to revisit the hip drop the following week.

That still gives you ten minutes to do some interesting walks. If, however, your students are great at hip drops too, then you will find yourself with an extra ten minutes. Return to the first move and add something to it, like flowing arms, or turn it into a travelling step. If the time is still on your side, try making up a short combo: walk, drop, walk, rotation. There are lots of ways to stretch or compress the material you want to teach. Be aware and ready to move on when, or preferably just before, the students seem to be getting bored or frustrated. Don't be afraid to keep them working on a move to help drill it into the muscle memory or so that you can walk the room to make adjustments.

Make a note on your lesson plan as to what got taught and how it was received. I usually just checkmark the lesson plan and pencil in if I added to it. Then when I am planning the class for next week I can see what needs to be revisited and where we left each move or combination.

Keep a close eye on the clock and try hard to stick to your plan. Some lessons will tempt you off onto a new subject, and it is up to you how much you let your mood or that of your students direct your lesson. If you do go totally off, plan to spend some time rewriting your term plan to prioritize what you still want to teach. It's not very professional to arrive in class and obviously try to shoehorn in a move that you forgot to teach them last week.

Sometimes you may want to spend your whole hour on a concept or activity, but it is still useful to fill out your lesson plan and stick to some structure. Here is a simple lesson plan for a session in which the students are going to write their own duet:

    0:00 – Meet and greet
    0:05 – Soft warm-up
    0:10 – Heart rate warm-up
    0:15 – Revisit suitable moves, including technique, combinations, or styling from last week
    0:20 – Outline activity, pick duet pairs; discuss lyrics and context of song. Send dancers to their space to start their planning
    0:25 – Check that everyone is happy; distribute pens and scrap paper and rough timings for their choreography
    0:30 – Remind the group of some ways to make duets look special: interaction, mirroring, question and answer, travelling, frames
    0:35 – Walk to each group in turn to assess and assist with their work
    0:40 – Ask if anyone has any questions or problems. Five-minute warning
    0:45 – Ask half the groups to perform for the others. Ask for feedback on what worked
    0:50 – The other half performs. More feedback
    0:55 – Cooldown

Although this lesson doesn't work with total beginners, it does work with almost any other kind of group and is the perfect lesson to have with you at all times. Have a playlist planned just in case you are ill or injured, which might mean you want to do less dancing in your lesson than usual. I find that the students enjoy the creative process, and their output can be very inspiring.

Providing students with a rough outline for their choreography can help dispel that initial fear of the blank three minutes ahead of them and also show them how you start on your own choreography work. I write out my rough outline to suit their level of knowledge.

This would work for students who have had about ten weeks of lessons:

0:00 – Opening – Violin, starts soft, builds
0:25 – 0:45 – Violin continues over regular drumbeat
0:45 – 1:05 – Drumbeat on its own
1:05–1:15 – Solo singer verse "Habibi."
1:15–1:35 – Solo singer chorus
1:35–1:55 – Backing singers repeat chorus
1:55–2:05 – Solo singer verse "Habibi."
2:05–2:25 – Backing singers repeat chorus, solo singer "Ahhhh."
2:25–2:45 – Drumbeat, backing singers repeat chorus
2:45–2:55 – Drumbeat only
2:55 – end – Violin to fadeout

Now, instead of having a blank three minutes, they have eleven sections of about twenty seconds each. Plus they can also see where they need the same or similar repeats of combinations, and they also know where I think the highlights should be. As the students' knowledge improves, you can name the drum patterns, point out more important words from the lyrics, and break the music into smaller sections. Or you may prefer the pleasure of watching them realize that they know more about the music than just the rough outline.

PICKING YOUR MUSIC

Your music will be very personal to you and will do a great deal to set the tone and mood of your lessons. It is incredibly hard to find music that appeals to everyone, but as a teacher it is your job to introduce new artists and sounds to your students while still keeping the lesson upbeat and accessible. I suggest that you plan music for each activity and then look at each lesson plan as a whole to see whether the music is too similar or too complex and tweak it accordingly. The perfect piece of music can make the difference between your students' understanding a move or feeling like a failure.

Music has many roles in a class setting, so you may find yourself purchasing music because it fulfills a need, even though you don't immediately love it. When purchasing a new album, I am on the lookout for music that fulfills my needs as a teacher:

Music to teach moves to

This music should be repetitive, with the beat or melody you want them to listen to coming through clearest or loudest and nice and clean. You don't want any breaks or stops, unless you know they are coming and you can use them to have a little shakedown or roll the shoulders back to release tension. Look for a mid-tempo to which the moves can be done at a comfortable speed. Not so slow that every muscle aches (although that is great for later classes!) and not so fast that the students don't have time to think about the movements. For sharp moves, look for something with a touch of pop that has a nice clear count of eight. For teaching soft moves, look for music with a repetitive melody and very little beat, or perhaps a soft beat that is low in the music mix. If you teach a soft move to a beat, you will have everyone breaking the move into eight counts and making it staccato. Again, that would be nice to teach later on or as a way to get everyone in time with each other for group choreography, but early on you want soft and smooth. Practice at home to your music and make sure any counts you will be using are clear.

Music to cross the floor

To get people travelling, you should look for music with a bit of a kick. Party music will help with smiles, and a beat will help the dancers place their feet. If you want a slinky travelling move, go still more upbeat than you would for stationary work, and give the dancers clear instructions on how to use the music to travel, or you may find they don't go anywhere. I like my travelling music to be very repetitive and long. You will find your class mood broken if you have to return to restart a track every three minutes. Music that's seven or eight minutes long works much better. It is useful if you can dance the combination at either half or full speed, so look for something with a good count that can also be called at half time: 12345678 and 1+2+3+4+5+6+7+8+.

Music every dancer should know

There are a number of CDs available with the "top ten" or "top 100" tracks that every belly dancer should know, and it is useful to introduce these to your dancers early on. You may have your own list of must-know music based on the style that you teach. Some of the classics are more complex than others, and complex music can be scary to new students, but it's also good to let your students know that not all belly dance music is eight-count pop. I use this kind of music a lot in my Ta-dah! section at the end of class, perhaps showing how a combination fits perfectly into the chorus of a belly dance classic or how we can mark a drumbeat with our hips. Keep your ears pricked for any of your top ten music that you can use to teach a basic move or concept nice and early on in the term, and be ready to tell your students why it's considered a classic and some of the background and history.

Arabic pop

Arabic pop can be the teacher's friend, if it fits into your style of belly dance. The beat tends to be nice and clear and the music is popular with students. Try to mix up your artists so you don't end up with one dominating your term, and look for tracks with Arabic highlights rather than music that could have come from anywhere in the world. Sneak in a few tracks that are Arabic reimaginings of songs that have recently been popular to see your students try to work out where they have heard it before.

Introducing instruments

Listen for music that will give you a chance to discuss the different instruments used in Arabic music. Taqsim are a wonderful way to do this, and a haunting nay taqsim can be used early on to mix up different-sized rotations or a variety of figure eights and introduce the idea that dancing is not just a shopping list of moves but a connection to the music and an emotional journey. This makes for a great Ta-dah! at the end of the lesson and can give students confidence as dancers early on to listen to the music and let their body flow.

Be aware of how much you, as a lover of belly dance, may have become attuned to the Arabic instruments and how you felt when you first heard them. Students can be turned off by excessive repetitive finger cymbals/zills or by a long track highlighting the mizmar or a particularly depressing oud. Try to find a short piece with the instrument clean and clear and then a couple of other pieces where that instrument gets short starring moments, so that they can become attuned to picking out the instruments in a busy, orchestrated track.

Drum patterns

There are now a number of great CDs on the market with clean drum patterns. Sometimes these are sold as teaching aids or as learn-to-play-drum packages. They make a great addition to every teacher's music library, focusing on simple or not-so-simple drum patterns. They are wonderful to teach the main drum patterns to but also to teach moves, combinations, and cross the floor. By their own design they can be one-dimensional, so I would avoid using more than one per lesson. After you have played the drum pattern from a teaching CD, it is useful to play another track with the same pattern at a similar tempo but orchestrated so that the students can hear the pattern in busier music. This makes for a good Ta-dah! moment.

I find it useful to play "invisible drum" along to the tracks so that the students can see what they are hearing. I am by no means a great drummer, but my invisible drum is very forgiving. Take time to explain the dum and tak tones and watch other drummers to see how they place their hands to make the different sounds. Ask your students to play the invisible drum with you or to clap or pace the patterns. If you have a group who are particularly foot motivated (they like to dance from their feet rather than their hips, or they always ask what their feet are doing, even with shoulder rolls), use the feet to mark the music and then use the natural swing of the hips to make a simple reflection of the pattern.

Warm-up and cooldown music

Your warm-up music will set the tone for the whole lesson, and your cooldown music will be the tune your students hum on their way home, so both are very important. I will write more about what to plan for both your warm-up and cooldown later, but for my soft warm-up I like to find something soft, welcoming, and uplifting, with a regular beat. Some students will be arriving late, some will be slow to make it to their spot, and I like to let them drift in on their own time. Some teachers like their students to be in place and ready to go; if you are one of these, choose an opening piece with a strong start. You will need to know this music very well so that you can run through your warm-up moves while still talking or covering safety tips. For my heart rate raiser I pick out a feel-good party tune, perhaps something that will surprise the students or put a smile on their faces. For the cooldown I like to find something more mellow and less led by a beat. Cooldown music still has to be warm and cheerful but can be more reflective and relaxing. If you like to end with a short meditation or deep breathing, make sure your music doesn't wind up toward the end or your playlist doesn't move on to a drum solo, just as your class is at its most relaxed.

Music for shimmies

The whole idea of shimmies can be very scary to students, who may have never asked their body to do anything remotely like a shimmy before and your music can go a long way toward helping their shimmies develop. The more tense dancers get about wanting to shimmy, the less likely they are to be able to do it. When choosing shimmy music, avoid anything that might make them panic or tense up. Find a regular beat at a good relaxed speed so you can regularly distract them with shoulder rolls or interesting arm work. As they become more confident, mix in music with a regular drum pattern that you can use to add another move (shimmy, shimmy, shimmy, dum, dum, dum.)

Music for improvisation

When introducing improvisation, it helps the dancers if they already know the music, so this would be my most western music selection. A number of artists have had worldwide success with music that the general public associates with belly dance. To your attuned ears it may not sound very belly dance, but many students start classes because they want to dance like the girl in the video for something popular. I also like to use the free dance time for music with a seasonal feel. Popular music is popular for a reason. Once your dancers have the idea of free dance in their minds, you can move them to music they have never heard but that is predictable. Then you can slowly move into less predictable music using the drum patterns they have learned or music that is similar to tracks they have used elsewhere in their lessons.

Music for group choreographies

The music you choose for your groups will be heard at least twice per lesson, and you may have to work on a section hundreds of times to get it right. It is therefore important that not only you love it, but your students love it too. They need to go on stage smiling even if they have dreamt about their music all night. Depending on where you are performing, you may have strict time restrictions that will limit your options, but try to find a few repetitive sections that can be taught early on and a few interesting parts to keep the audience's attention. Decide what kind of opening and finish you want your performance to have and which of your dancers' skills you want to highlight.

I am always looking for new music to add to my mix, but I also like to have some favorites that I know are great for teaching certain moves. I keep a long list of moves and combinations, and each time I buy a new album I listen to see how many of the tracks I can use. I instantly list each track as a possible warm-up, cooldown, shimmy, move, improvisation, group number, combo, or solo performance – or unusable. Some music is so special that it begs for a new combination or topic all its own; maybe it is inspiring you towards fan veils or shaabi. Sometimes a track can be so special that it is worth marking it for future use even if it doesn't fit into any of the topics you are currently working on. Who hasn't suddenly needed a saiidi techno tune with an upbeat violin solo?

Most music software will let you tag or put a note on your music; I do this so it is easier to search at a later date, or you can simply put a postcard into your CD case. You may have dismissed a track as unusable on first listen and then find yourself desperate for a drum solo with some nay (flute) later in the term, so note down all your thoughts even if they seem irrelevant. As you use music in class, you will find out what is working and what isn't. I keep a playlist of solid, basic tracks that give me the option to swap tracks if something new isn't working.

I also keep hundreds of playlists for specialty music, from styles and instruments to a fast regular beat or music that makes me feel melancholy. You never know what your students might ask for, and it's good to have music you can go to right away to give an example. Finally, prepare a playlist of your most trusted music to put on your phone or on a CD in your purse in case you ever have to teach a lesson or perform unexpectedly or without your bag of necessities.

Once you have allocated your existing music selections, this will give you some ideas for the music you are missing, and there are many online communities happy to point you to some good CDs to help fill your library. To save money, I suggest that new teachers look for "best of" albums and start off fairly pop-focused so that they can be sure that every track they buy can be used, or buy online from a supplier who will sell each track individually. Traders at belly dance events are usually very knowledgeable and stock the CDs that they know will sell. Don't be tempted to "borrow" music from other teachers (to make copies) or buy bootlegged music. The early teachers of belly dance used to teach using four or five LPs, and you should be able to do the equivalent with CDs until your classes are making enough money for you to reinvest in your business.

Practical Tip:
Pick a CD off your shelf and listen to it while making a note of what each track would be most suited to. Repeat with all your other belly dance CDs.

HOW DO PEOPLE LEARN?

In the last few years a huge amount of research has gone into understanding how people learn. When I was in school we were told a fact and maybe asked to write it out ten times or to place it in a sentence or to use a highlighter to help us remember. Think about dates or places from your history lessons at school. Do you remember the ones that you pinned to your bedroom walls or the rhyme that your teacher made up? Perhaps, like me, you don't remember any of these!

We are really lucky in teaching belly dance over other subjects. First, it helps that all our students want to be there and have chosen this as a subject they are interested in. Second, we are not teaching toward an exam or within a limited curriculum, so we can pick topics that inspire us and take our time to make sure everyone has a good idea of what we want them to learn. Third, we can constantly evolve and adapt how and what we teach to suit our students and their learning styles.

In my experience, very few people fall into a single and clearly defined, consistant learning style. More typically, we switch between styles from week to week, lesson to lesson, and concept to concept. Even if you feel that you know how your students learn best, it is worth considering each learning style and providing some time for each approach to cater to everyones needs. If a student doesn't seem to understand a move or concept, step back and consider all the learning styles and how to teach to them:

- Show the move
- Explain the move
- Build a story around the move
- Count the move
- Break down the move
- Explain why we do the move
- Move the student (gently but firmly)

LEARNING STYLES

The Visual Learner

Visual learners learn by watching. They see the body move and can understand that movement and echo that movement with their own body. They may need to see the move from the front, back, or side. They often understand the whole movement better than the component parts, so they will move their arms, hips, and feet just as you did without needing the weight shift or the arm pattern explained. They feel confident following behind you as you dance but often struggle with improvisation or dancing without you to lead. Sometimes they subconsciously leave out an important part of the move, such as engaging the abs, because they didn't see it happen. They are good at learning from videos and shows but not so good at explaining what they are doing to others.

The Audio Learner

Audio learners work best with spoken instructions. They hear what you want them to do and can turn those instructions into a movement. They may need a real-life story to explain the movement, such as "Imagine you are petting a hamster that is stuck on the top of a cupboard" or a more detailed explanation: "Reach your arm up, but keep your shoulder down, soften your elbow slightly but keep the arm long. Flex though your middle finger, letting the other fingers follow and keep your wrist relaxed so that it rolls back and forth with the movement." Audio learners hate it when we say "Do this, then this, a doodah and a dum." And they get frustrated when we teach without reference to the music or simply count past the interesting musical variation. They love

it if the combinations fit the music perfectly, and they are the first to point out that the drummer hits his drum slightly harder the third time in the repeat. Their free dance is often filled with beautiful nuances.

The Verbal Learner

Verbal learners like to repeat instructions back at you or take notes to reinforce the information. "Did you just say three to the left?" If it is inappropriate for them to simply echo your words, they may verbalize them in the form of questions or by mouthing the count, nodding, or taking notes. It often takes courage to write down notes in a dance class, so don't discourage them. They like to sing along to the music or to make up rhymes to help remember the combination: "Down, down, wiggle, wiggle, step, tap, bounce, bounce." Beware of this if you are a verbal learning teacher, as your students will get very grumpy when they discover that "wiggle" covers a multitude of moves depending on what combination they are

learning. It would be far better for you to call the moves by a set name even if they don't fit as well with the music. Verbal dancers may find it hard to resist mouthing the count even when on stage, so make sure they don't rely on this practice once the choreography is in their head, or give in to their need to make noise to animate the face.

The Logical Leaner

Logical learners need to gather all the facts before they start to dance. They like to know the foot pattern, weight shifts, muscle groups, angle of the chest, speed of the hips, and arm-to-leg balance, lines, and eye focus. They also need to know about the music, the reason we are learning this combination, the mood of the piece, how it would feel to watch this performance, how big the stage will be, and what costumes we will be wearing.

Some logical learners are best taught from the feet up, or hip first; other logical learners need to see the whole choreography before they can start on the first move. I like to think of these two subtypes as the minute logical learner and the whole picture logical learner. If you have these two extremes in the class, it is almost impossible to please everyone, but you can try.

The minute logical learner wants to start with one part of one move; the whole picture logical learner wants to know how this first move is going to work in the overall choreography. It is good for you to have a whole picture idea in your head before you start so that you can paint a picture of the big idea; for example:

"This is a number for our stage show. I want us to fill the stage with lots of big movements, lines, circles, and interlocking diamonds. I don't want the audience to be able to pick out particular dancers. I want each of you to be lost in the chaos, but then to suddenly be a tidy shape for the drum section. We are like a flock of birds who have been disturbed, finding our own shape again. The arms are going to have to be perfect, and I am going to expect you all to be able to travel from one position to the next without breaking the combinations. We will learn this combination travelling left, right, forward, and back, so that each time you have to move you can be confident with where you are going and not worry about the feet."

The Physical Learner

Physical learners need to feel the moves. It is because of this learning style that I ask everyone to agree, in the waiver they sign, to the use of touch as a teaching method. Sometimes it is necessary to stand in front of the student, have her put her hands on your hips, and do the move slowly and as large as you can so that she can feel the movement.

I also invite the dancers to touch their own bodies as they dance to feel where the movements are coming from. The most obvious example is during tummy work, when the movements may be too small to see in the mirror and looking down changes the posture and the way the abs work. Simply placing her hands on her tummy during tummy work helps a student to understand the movements and repeat them. Putting the hands on the gluteus or abs during many hip moves can help the physical learner understand the part these muscles play in not only powering a move but also keeping her steady, balanced, and contained.

Physical learners also respond better to having their arms or hands adjusted by touch than to hearing you explain that they are too soft or too straight. Be aware of how often you touch your students and how they react to your touch. Some people are extremely sensitive or find touch difficult emotionally, so be on the lookout for body language warning signs. By including this issue in your waiver, you have already made it acceptable. I try to start my walking of the room to make adjustments with a student I know well or who is open to touch. Always ask before you touch any area between knees and shoulders.

Sometimes physical learners are eager to understand the muscle groups, so be prepared to explain exactly which muscle is doing what and how the others support the movement. It can be very tempting with the physical learner to push her around from one position to the next in group choreography, but she learns better by figuring out her own route, even if you take her hand for the first few run-throughs. Try bringing a chess set to class so that each dancer can move her piece around the board a few times in time to the music before trying it on the dance floor.

The Emotional Learner

Emotional learners truly dance from the heart right from the very first lesson. Sometimes they dance to their own inner tune or to tell their own story. They can be difficult to teach because they are not very interested in muscles or counts and have just come to dance class to dance. Although it is rare to have a totally emotional learner, it is not unusual to have a dancer switch over to the emotional style for a few weeks. Be careful how you correct the emotional learner; keep her safe, but also be quick to reinforce her when she does the move perfectly. Sometimes the emotional dancer has a whole story or fantasy life created on which she builds her dancing, and she can be magical to watch. She may offer up some stunning, creative ways to improve on a choreography, and it is always worth listening, but don't let the whole group get  distracted for too long. Examine your own feelings as you dance and share those with the class as a whole to show that emotion plays a big part in what makes this dance special.

TEACHING TO EACH STYLE OF LEARNER

Before getting into the details of teaching moves, let us look again at how we teach to each learner's needs. As I've said:

- Show the move
- Explain the move
- Build a story around the move
- Count the move
- Break down the move
- Explain why we do the move
- Move the student

Now we should consider how teaching to each learning style works within the studio.

When showing the move, consider how it looks to the students, and position yourself so that everyone can see you. That may mean standing on a stage, making use of a mirror, or moving around the room repeating the move. Even with small, neat moves, keep them large enough to be seen easily. It may be necessary to add an arm movement that is about guiding the eyes rather than a dance arm move. For example, when teaching tummy rolls you will need to point to your abs as they move in and out, but it might also be useful to move your fingers away and toward your tummy as you roll to show which muscles are moving in and out.

When we explain the move, we link it to other moves, to styles of dance and uses in performance. We might talk about how a move has a common shape with other moves, travels in a really useful way, or is a key part of a traditional folk dance. Giving the students an overview motivates them to learn the move and drill it until it is perfect.

Building a story around a move helps with visualization and also with remembering the moves when it comes to free dance. A hip drop may not be the way most teenage girls bounce their hip while talking to their mothers, but that's a strong visual and emotional hook that most people can instantly connect with. It also reminds our students that this movement is something they know and can do in a relaxed and slightly humorous way (arms crossed, face full of attitude), which is only a small step away from being able to do in a dance setting.

Counting the move is affected by your music choice, but in simple terms it is counting from the beginning of the bar until the end. In most pop music that count will be:

12345678

If you would like your dancers to slow a move down, you can either only call the odd numbers:

1 3 5 7

or call your 1 to 8 over a 16 count with a plus ("and") between each when nothing happens:

1+2+3+4+5+6+7+8

In Arabic music I prefer to call the music by its dum and taks. That might be a saiidi beat:

Dum tak dum dum tak

Before you use a dum and tak, explain how they work to your dancers and either show them how you would play a dum and a tak on a drum, or give a demonstration with an invisible drum.

I find that the music dictates which counting style I go with, and it's OK to mix them as long as your count fits the music:

"Shimmy! 2345678, dum tak dum dum tak, dum dum and dum!"

Breaking down the move involves not only a deep understanding of how a move works but also skill in explaining that to the students. Take some time before you teach class to fully understand each move of the dance, how it links to others, and how each part of the body interacts to make it happen. Think about the weight shift in feet, where the pressure hits the ankles and knee joints, where the strength and motion comes from, and which muscles are working hard to make it happen. Look for anticipating moves, or the moves that prepare the body for the featured move, and the ways your body reacts to maintain balance and momentum. Feel the stresses and pulls on your body, the diagonal reactions and the control needed to isolate. Notice which muscles tense, which relax, and in what order. These minute details are what will help your dancers move as you do and will also help you to understand why some people struggle with a move while it comes to others easily. The trick in teaching this way is to give enough information so that the move is done easily and in the right way, but not so much that the students are overwhelmed and too busy thinking about their muscle control to relax and allow a move to flow. Start with the most important features of each move and then add more information slowly until everyone in the room is doing it the way you want them to.

Explaining why we are doing a move again motivates the students and helps them to link moves together. This is why I like my end-of-lesson Ta-dah! moment, when all the moves are used together to produce an end product that makes sense of all the hard work. You can simply say "This is my favorite move," and that is a good enough reason to teach it. Or you might tell the students how they are going to build on that move over the next few weeks, or how you want it to be strong so that they can shimmy over it or so you can add it to their choreography.

Taking hold of a student and physically moving her should be used rarely and with delicacy and respect. None of your students should ever need pushing around, but a gentle guiding hand can sometimes do more than a thousand words. A gentle touch on the shoulders can make a student remember to relax; a forearm across the knees can remind her not to pump her knees too much. Let your students feel how you move, but again, always ask for permission before touching them between the knees and shoulders. It can be great fun to split your group into pairs to put their hands on each other's tummies during tummy rolls, but be sensitive and allow them to find their own partners or to opt out of that exercise.

Later on I will give you some pointers on how to teach those important few beginners moves, but first I want to break down the whole teaching process using just one move. I am going to use an outward, vertical figure eight that I call a maya in my classes. This move goes by many names, and is also sometimes called a cobra. I will explain what I say and do and who that part of the lesson is aimed at and why. Before I teach a maya, I like my students to be confident with a horizontal figure eight.

As you read what's happening, recall the different learning styles and see whether you can identify which style each teaching approach would particularly connect with. Note that many of the methods are effective with multiple learning styles.

The following is a minute, chronological breakdown for teaching the maya.

Introduction: "Today we are going to do a beautiful move in the figure eight family."

Explain: "Last week we did this horizontal figure eight."

Show: Horizontal figure eight, half time.

Why: "I'm keeping it smooth and horizontal, but today's move, the maya, tips the figure eight on its side and looks very different to the audience."

Show: Maya, half time.

Explain: "We did the figure eight parallel to the floor."

Show: Draw a figure eight with a flat palm in front of the body.

Explain: "The maya is still that eight or infinity shape but drawn toward the audience or parallel to the mirror."

Show: Wave arm in an infinity shape toward the mirror.

Story: "It's more like you are polishing the mirror, rather than polishing the floor."

Breakdown: "We start off with our good posture: feet, knees, hips, tummies, chest, shoulders, chin, and smile."

Teaching a Maya - A step-by-step breakdown for various learning styles, cont.

Show: Good posture.

Story: "Just like the infinity and the figure eight, they have no start and no finish, but we have to start them somewhere, and I have decided we start in our good posture and then travel our hips to the right."

Breakdown: "So while keeping our feet totally flat, we are going to tighten up our abs and bum, but only on the right side."

Show: Point to right abs and right bum cheek.

Breakdown: "Now keeping those muscles tight, we are going to slide the hips over to the right, but keep the shoulders lined up over our feet."

Show: Slide the hips to your right (or left if you are facing the group).

Story: "Don't take your shoulders with you, or you look like you want to lean on the bus stop!"

Show: Lean your body and then repeat the hip slide with the shoulders in place to reinforce how you want the move done.

Count: "This is the first part of the move."

Why: "And it's OK to let this move flow along at its own speed if that's how the melody is speaking to us." (Especially useful for the emotional learner.)

Count: "We can also let the beat guide us, which is what we are going to do to begin with." **Breakdown:** "From this position we are going to gradually release the hip down toward the floor, but nice and controlled."

Show: Controlled drop.

Count: "This is the second part of our move."

Breakdown: "From here, this bottom right corner, we are going to start to lift the hip with the left abs and glutes and slide the hip over to the top left corner."

Show: Diagonal slide.

Count: "At this top left corner we have our third count."

Breakdown: "And then we control the drop down to the bottom left."

Show: Drop hip on left.

Count: "For the fourth and final part of the move . . ."

Breakdown: "This time we are going to start where we are: this bottom left corner and slide up to the right, drop down, up to the left, drop down."

Show: Slow broken maya.

Count: "1, 2, 3, 4."

Story: "This gives us a kind of bow tie shape."

Show: Draw a bow tie shape with your hands toward the mirror.

Story: "It's like walking up the side of a hill and then falling off the cliff. Diagonally up and then straight down, diagonally up the other side and straight down a cliff the other side."

Explain: "But we want something more like the infinity shape."

Show: Draw an infinity shape with your hands toward the mirror.

Story: "We are not moving the hips forward and back at all; it's as if we got caught between two panes of glass and can only move sideways."

Teaching a Maya - A step-by-step breakdown for various learning styles, cont.

Breakdown: "We are going to get that shape by focusing on using the muscles to give a controlled lift and release, smoothing out the corners and making the flow look effortless."

Why: "To begin with this feels really odd, because we don't usually move or stretch in this direction. The horizontal figure eight comes naturally to lots of us as a way we sway to music."

Story: "But we do use this movement in real life, just not very often. I would like you to think for a moment about stepping over a log but without moving your feet . . ."

Move: "Put your hands on your hip bones . . ."

Show: Put your hands on your hip bones.

Story: "And imagine you have a low fence or a fallen log to your right."

Breakdown: "Lift your right leg and put your foot the other side of the log. Feel what happened to your hip."

Show: Step sideways over an imaginary log.

Breakdown: "Feel how you lifted your hip with your foot, and then slid it to the right while you were reaching for the other side and finally dropped your hip down as you placed your foot."

Story: "Lift your foot, take it over the log, stretch for the other side, and place your foot down."

Show: Step over the imaginary log as slowly as you can.

Breakdown: "Now do the same on the other side. Lift the foot and the hip, stretch over to the other side and slide the hip, place the foot on the ground and drop the hip.

Move: "Can you feel how your hips are moving during that movement?"

Teaching a Maya - A step-by-step breakdown for various learning styles, cont.

Story: "So now all we have to do is step sideways over a log, but just without moving our feet."

Count: "1, 2, 3, 4."

Show: Fluid maya.

Why: "This move is smaller than it looks. It is much better to have that control than to overstretch or try to make it look big. It is already impressive. Focus on keeping the moves tight and the rest of the body isolated. There is a real temptation to lift the heels, and that is OK with me if you want to make the move bigger – say, on a big stage or to show a variation – but let's start off small and controlled."

Show: Small, controlled maya.

Story: "I really struggled with this move. Then I practiced every time I made a phone call. I started out really small, but it didn't take long before I got more flexible, and you can do hundreds of these during a nice, chatty phone call."

Explain: "OK, let's add music. We will start with that bow tie shape and break the move down into a count of four, and then we will work on softening the corners, isolating the rest of the body, and keeping it soft and fluid."

Show: Use your hand to make the shapes you want.
Add music with a slow regular beat for about thirty seconds and then an interesting, slow melody.

Count: "1, 2, 3, 4."

Story: "Uphill, off cliff, uphill, off cliff."

Breakdown; "Diagonally up, straight down, diagonally up, straight down, right, down, left, down."

Teaching a Maya - A step-by-step breakdown for various learning styles, cont.

Show: Slow bow tie shape maya.

Breakdown: "Now soften the corners. Watch the upper body and keep your heels down."

Explain: "This is such a pretty move, but it doesn't need to look like a stretch. Keep it small."

At this point, walk the room making corrections. Unless someone is going to injure herself, focus on one correction per person. Look out for bad posture, hips twisting forward and back, overstretching, moving too fast, heels lifting, working the move from the knees, shoulders joining in, head moving from side to side, counting out loud, ugly arms or hands, and tension.

Move: "Put your hands on my hips and follow me."

Show: Allow the students each to stand behind you and put their hands on your hip bones. Do your maya very slowly and with lots of control. When you feel them moving in time with you, take a half step forward so they can continue and you can turn to look.

Move: "I'm just going to put my hands on your hips and ease them around in this maya shape. Just relax and let me slide them for you."

Show: Kneel down an arm's reach from their hips and show your hands moving the infinity shape a couple of inches from their body, then lightly touch their hips with your fingertips, allowing them to follow your hands with their hips.

Explain: "That was looking nice. I would like you to try and practice that move for a few minutes each day if you can. It's really one of those moves that takes a little time to get control over, but it's so worth it."

You may not agree with the way I teach mayas, but I hope you can see how each learning style is taught. I showed the move to the visual learner, I explained the move for the audio learner, I counted out the move for the verbal learner, I broke down the move for the logical learner, I moved the physical learner, and I set up stories for the emotional learner. As noted earlier, many of the things I said or did were aimed at more than one type of learning style, keeping in mind that most people learn using a mix of styles.

Practical Tip:

Follow this chapter as a script and act it out as if you were teaching a class, either in front of a mirror or videotaping yourself. Which bits felt natural, and which didn't work? Can you explain the move better than I did? What stories can you use from your own life? How do you count a maya? How would you break it down? Why do you love (or hate) this move?

Practical Tip:

In front of the mirror or a video camera, teach your pretend class how to do a simple circle or hip rotation. Write out everything you said or did and decide which learning styles it addresses. Did you show the move, explain the move, tell a story, count the move, break it down, talk about why we do this move, or physically move your student? Which learning styles do you naturally teach toward? Did you cover something for everyone? Which of the learning styles needs more attention from you?

Practical Tip:

Continue with filming or teaching to the mirror. Can you teach a hip drop or hip down for just one learning style? Start with the visual learner, then tailor your style for the audio learner, verbal learner, logical learner, physical learner, and finally the emotional learner. Which was the easiest for you to do? Which style of learning do you find it hard to teach toward?

Practical Tip:

Attend a class or workshop and ask to be allowed to sit at the back to take notes. What learning style does the teacher prefer to focus on? What learning styles work best with each student? How many repeats of instructions did it take for each student to "get it"? How early in the lesson can you spot the learning styles of particular students? What learning style works best with the majority of the students? How do the classmates react to the dancers with a less popular learning style?

To visualize how we learn any new subject imagine stairs cut into a hill side. Sometimes the step up is small, other times it is a knee height. Sometimes the steps are close together and other times we walk a few paces between the steps. Our path to learning belly dance is not smooth and even; improvements may come straight after an increased effort, or may take months as new information is processed. Each of your students will have a different reaction to new information, drills, explanations and demonstrations, but keep their focus on their goals and they will continue to move forward.

ORGANIZING YOUR TEACHING SPACE

How you organize your teaching space will depend on what your space is like and how flexible it allows you to be. I suggest that if you have a mirror you set that as the front of your room and teach from a center point in front of it so that students get an excellent view of you from all angles.

Before settling on which way to face in the space, look at electric outlets and where you can place your music system and lesson plan. You don't want to have to walk through your students every time you want to press pause in your music. Check the room lighting; you want your teaching position to be either in a spotlight or at least as well lit as the rest of the room. Finally, estimate how many people are going to attend and walk the room, checking how good the view is going to be for them from different spots.

Before your students arrive, organize your table so that everything is accessible without looking cluttered. I like to have three zones: my work station, with sound system and lesson plan; the check-in area, with register and cash box; and the student resources area, with handouts and goods for sale.

Your sound system must be near an outlet, and the speakers should face the room. Be aware that if you constantly move in front of the speakers, you will block the sound to the dancers, which can become annoying. Have the music systems controls next to your lesson plan, so you can check your notes as you adjust or pause the music. You will need to take sips of water throughout the lesson to help your voice, but don't place it where you need to reach across your sound system, in case you spill the water.

If you have coin belts or music for sale, place them on a different table or away from your lesson plan so that students can shop without blocking you from important paperwork or feeling like you are looking over their shoulder. You may also wish to put handouts and flyers on that table to attract interest and make them accessible.

Put your register, a pen, and your cashbox nearby. If you have a waiver or a welcome handout, place these within reach.

Be aware of first impressions as the students walk into the room for the first time. They are expecting to see a belly dance class, so if you set up where they can't see you, they may worry they have arrived at the wrong room and simply leave. Be careful not to set up in such a way that anyone arriving late comes in facing all the other students, which can be intimidating. Greeting them with a table of coin belts for sale, or all the other students' bags and coats, may not set the right tone either. They should be able to "get" the space and picture their place in it from the outset. I like to put on some soft music that is obviously belly dance so that they hear the class as they approach and know they are heading in the right direction.

Once you've gotten to know your students a bit, when organizing them into smaller groups or partners, take time before the lesson to think about what each of them needs. Will the lady who is really skilled but not assertive take charge of the bossy beginner or lose confidence by working with her? Will the lady with the huge hip lifts shrink hers to match her partner when she sees how small he makes his, or will they just look mismatched? Try to be fair and even-handed in your allocation of partners or subsets. Don't put the same people together week after week, and don't always pick the same team captains. Splitting the groups by what they are wearing, or by birthday month, seems fair. I like to split my beginners class by first name; that way they have to sort themselves out, and everyone gets to learn a name or two while they do it.

"Abby will start the lineup by the mirror, and Zoe will be at the other end by the door."

Some teachers find that splitting up their groups by astrological sign gets interesting results!

As you walk the room, look for groups that work and don't work and try to see why. Sometimes you can interject and quickly change the tone of the group. Maybe the one taking charge needs reminding that the aim was for each group member to suggest a move for the combo, not just one person.

FACING THE CROWD

Once you have your room organized, your table set up, your music selected, and your lesson plan written, it is time to come face-to-face with your students. This can be very daunting if you have not had any experience in public speaking or addressing groups of people.

Your students are looking to you not only to impart wisdom but also to run the lesson, improve their fitness, find them friends, and teach them to dance. You may be able to read all this from their expectant eyes, or you may be looking at a sea of bored faces. Sadly, not all students understand a teacher's need for bright eyes, attention, and occasional nods. Instead, they relax and stare at you as if you were the TV screen in the corner, letting your words of wisdom wash over them. A first-time teacher can panic at this point, asking too many questions, raising her voice, and moving around to try and motivate her class. Don't worry; remember to keep calm and stay in control. Trust in your lesson plan and the balance you have found between hard work and fun for your classes.

Make sure to ask all your new students about their level and experience when they start, and watch them as they warm up with you. It should be fairly simple to notice the dancers who are already confident with the posture, have strong arms, follow the music, and show belly dance technique. It is perfectly fine to ask a new student if she can do some moves, but it's probably better to phrase it in a way that shows that you are observant and interested in her and her journey; for example, "I see you have already taken some belly dance lessons. Who did you study with? Have you ever performed? What are you hoping to improve? What do you want to get out of these lessons?"

As your students relax during the warm-up, they may frown, nibble fingernails, or bite their lips. During drills their eyebrows may move in time to the moves and they may scrunch up their noses. Never, ever laugh at the funny faces you can see as you stand at the head of the room! This is our secret as belly dance teachers. Of course you want nice relaxed smiling faces when they appear on stage, but that may be some time in the future. While people are deep into learning, their faces take on a whole new vocabulary of expressions.

Belly dancers have a wonderful ability to read body language, and it can be off-putting to see the disappointment and shoulders dropping as you announce a seven-minute shimmy. But what did you expect? When you see the eyes roll at another repeat of the choreography, it may be time to call it "one last time," but if you need them to get the timing right, they may have to repeat that section two dozen more times. The payoff is the moment when they know that they have perfected that combination.

We haven't talked too much about positivity and negativity, but there are always going to be some people who brighten up the whole room and others who can crush a happy mood with just one look. Teaching is a very giving profession. You have to bring all your happiness, energy, and enthusiasm to the room every single time you teach and give it to each and every student without any expectation. This can be very draining, both physically and emotionally. You may have spent hours writing a choreography only to have one student say "It's kind of dull," or you may have hand washed your personal veil collection and packed them up, ready to share with your class, to be greeted by "Not veils again!" You must be prepared for this; don't let a few throwaway comments negatively impact your teaching.

You have been blessed with the opportunity to share a beautiful dance style with people in your community, to open up the world of dancing, to introduce a fascinating culture and sprinkle their workaday lives with sparkles. Don't let occasional negativity move you from your pathway. Of course, it's a good idea to get feedback at the end of each course and to tailor the classes to fit your students' needs, but a stray comment may have more to do with the dancer's bad day than with your teaching style.

None of us can hope to be the perfect teacher for everyone, but you can be the best that you are capable of being. Young students at a gym may want someone offering a more fitness-focused dance class, whereas the senior center students may want to have time to talk about their own experiences in the Middle East. You cannot suddenly increase your own stamina nor go back in time to spend your early twenties performing on a dinner boat on the Nile. However, you can add in an extra fun drill or focus more on crossing the floor for the gym class, and you can schedule five minutes at the beginning of class for show-and-tell with the seniors.

Each class will take on its own personality, but don't try to reinvent yourself over and over. It is striking that teachers seem to attract students who are very like themselves. Where a teacher is luxuriantly cuddly, students of a similar shape feel happy and accepted. The glamorous teachers have glamorous students. The tattooed troupes form around a tattooed teacher. Teachers may point out the diversity in their student base, and it is a reflection on how welcoming they are that not everyone feels they must conform, but you may also lose some dancers simply because you don't look like their idea of a belly dancer, or teach the style that attracted them to the dance. Be strong in who you are, and the right students will find you.

Teachers have to take control of their class and steer their students through the activities in the plan. We all remember from school the teachers who were screamers, the mad ones, the mice, and a few whom we loved and respected. You must earn your students' respect; arriving well prepared and with confidence will go a long way toward that goal. We are working mostly with adults, and they list "fun" as one of their main goals each and every time we ask. For some people, chatting with their new friends is fun; for others, the chatter can be annoying. Find your own balance between allowing them to share their newfound love of belly dance and continuing with the learning.

Show the dancers that you are ready to work by standing in position or by starting the music. I find a loud "Ladies and gentlemen!" said in a cut glass English accent is the best way to get their attention, but a zagreet is stylish. You can bring humor into the class by wagging a finger or using classic teacher phrases such as "If you have finally finished . . ." or "Would you like to share that with the class?" Finally, silence can be the loudest sound in a class. Waiting quietly at the front or putting your finger to your lips will attract their attention and make your point. Always follow class discipline with a smile or a joke to lighten the mood. Remind them that everyone has more fun when you are running the show.

POSTURE, POSTURE, POSTURE

Teaching posture is about more than just repeating a list of body parts in the hope that students will adjust themselves. It means constantly watching your students as they go through each movement, watching them walk and stand, their bodies in motion and stationary, and their balance points, weight shifts, and symmetry.

Each body is unique, and as we age we all fall into bad habits or have life dramas that affect our posture. Belly dance teachers have the chance to help dancers correct their posture, but we also have to work with students whose postural issues are a long-term project rather than an easy fix, or whose life has changed their body in such a way that they can never attain "perfect posture" as seen in the textbooks.

I'm going to talk here about the posture that I was taught and that I teach in class. You may wish to teach something slightly different if you have a back ground in yoga, or another dance style, but remember that your dancers may be older or less fit than those attending other kinds of classes. It is especially important to explain posture using all the different learning styles.

Feet should be making good contact with the floor, neither turned out nor lined up, and less than hip width apart. Beware of ladies who think they have enormous hips. I say that they need to leave just enough room for me to place one of my feet between theirs. At this point, look at ankles. Some people put the weight of their legs on either the outside or inside of their feet, so their ankles slant inward or outward. The person may be able to adjust this by either taking a small step in or out so that her feet are directly under her weight, or by focusing on keeping the whole weight-bearing sole of the foot (not the arch) in contact with the floor. People who are gripping the floor with their toes do not feel balanced; they need to adjust their foot width to feel safe, or balance the symmetry in another part of their body.

Knees should be "off lock," slightly soft, and aligned with the feet. We take the knees off lock to help with flexibility through the hips and to stop excess wear and tear on the knee joints. Some dancers will want to bend their knees, but this will work the thighs too hard and put extra pressure on the knees to keep the dancer balanced.

Pelvic floor should be engaged. You may want to phrase this in another way that suits your teaching, but I have never had any trouble or misunderstanding from referring to the pelvic floor muscles. Don't forget that men have pelvic floor muscles too and dance better with them engaged. Most women have heard about taking their pelvic floor "up in the elevator," and I say that if their pelvic floor lift goes all the way up to eight floors, for belly dance we want it on about the fourth floor. Maintaining an engaged pelvic floor is not easy for many people and there is no way we can check that they are doing it or help them make corrections. They should know that a strong pelvic floor doesn't just help with dancing or building core muscles; many women with stress incontinence have been helped by the pelvic floor strengthening of belly dancing. You may never experience this yourself, but I assume that for every woman who has told me that I have changed her life by helping with this embarrassing problem, there are half a dozen more who never told me. Chances are that you will have someone in your class who needs to tone up her pelvic floor, so take the time in each class to remind them until it becomes habit. It is a potentially life-changing gift.

Hips should be tilted slightly forward. This often happens with the engaging of the pelvic floor or the lower abs or the gluteus. Look out for students who hear "tilt" and instead push their hips forward (like the front of a hip rotation), taking them out of line with their shoulders and feet. Some teachers prefer to describe this as "lengthening the back," but I find that makes dancers stand tall by lifting their shoulders rather than straightening their tail bone. If you are confident with your students, you can ask them to run a finger down their spine and see how their tail bone moves as they tilt. Most of us stand with our tail out like a Tyrannosaurus rex, but tipping the hips makes the tail bone point more toward the ground. Be aware of which body part is hips and which is bottom (or bum, as we say in the UK). Teachers always want me to tip my hips more, because I have a very round bottom that still looks more "out" when I tilt than most people's bottoms look when they are in poor posture.

Ribs should be lifted. It is important that you define the area that you mean and the direction in which you want them to go. I talk about the chest area, but to some students that is their breasts, which are near impossible to lift on their own. The ribs and chest area need to lift straight up, lengthening the spine. The dancer should not be leaning back or forward, so you will need to look at her from the side as well as facing you. Remind students not to use their breath to lift, but instead engage their abs and lower back. Most of us lift our chest each day as we try to fasten our bra at the back.

Shoulders should roll back and down. Shoulders are often up at this point in class, as tension is reflected in the body. I like dancers to roll their shoulders backward a couple of times before stopping at the lowest point they reach while circling backward. This posture is very awkward for some students, particularly those with large breasts who have always brought their shoulders forward to hide or shrink their bustline. It does feel very much like you are thrusting your breasts forward if you are not used to standing like this. I think it is better to acknowledge that awkwardness at this point and reassure then that it will feel natural, given time.

Elbows should be pointing to the back corners of the room. By moving the elbows outward we create a space between the body and the arms. Some teachers tell their students to keep an imaginary tennis ball in each armpit, but that can lead to a "henchman hunch" and tension in the shoulders. If you have mirrors, the students can see their arms making a more circular shape.

Wrists and hands should be slightly lifted so that the inside of the wrist, where you might dab perfume, is elongated. Some older adults lose flexibility in their wrists, so do not force this position.

Fingers should be arched slightly away from the palm, with the middle finger slightly dipped. You can describe this in many ways, but I like my students to imagine holding a marble between their middle finger and thumb. This hand position not only looks nice but also reflects the hand position needed to play finger cymbals. If the other three fingers "flop" they will touch the edge of the cymbals and deaden the note, so they all stay arched and slightly tense.

Each man is different in how he likes his hands to be styled, but I give them the option of dipping the middle finger only slightly as if holding a tennis ball. On a larger man this can makes the hand look more in proportion.

Neck should be long, as an extension of the long back. You may find that pushing the shoulders down while also elongating the neck can cause stretching and tension, so build toward a long neck over the course of a few months rather than forcing it too quickly. Watch for people who bring their shoulders up toward their ears and those who raise their chin rather than the whole head when asked to elongate the neck.

Chin should be slightly lifted. This is a personal choice and changes as you add character to your dance, but I find this helps with the long body line. Dropping the chin can lead to a chain reaction that runs down the body, releasing all the other elements of the posture.

Smile should be natural, with some teeth showing.

Once you have your dancers in this posture, look at them face on and from different angles. Check how they distribute their weight between their feet and that their shoulders, hips, and feet are in alignment. Look for a soft, natural curve in the spine and an even symmetry between the halves of the body. Check that their muscles are on alert – that is, ready for action – rather than tense, and that they look comfortable.

When you see something out of line, it is quickest and easiest to simply ask the student if she has issues or is aware of injuries. These sometimes don't show in the expected area; for example, an injured shoulder may push the hip out of alignment. Being aware of posture problems can be all it takes for a dancer to make a good correction that may help with her whole life. If your correction doesn't seem to work or the student doesn't know of any issues, suggest she mention it to her doctor next time she has a visit. Women who carry children on their hip tend to be very one-sided, so you could suggest they shift the child to the other side more often. I also see many people who grow stronger on the side they habitually carry a heavy school bag or purse. Suggesting they switch to a daypack (and using both straps) can make them aware of the problems they may be causing themselves long term.

EFFECTIVE WARM-UPS

Your warm-up has a number of aims:

- To help you identify any injuries or limitations in your students
- To set the tone of the class
- To lubricate joints
- To relax nervous students
- To provide a workout
- To prepare the mind and body for the class
- To prepare or warm up the muscle sets to be used in class
- To release adrenaline into the body
- To gently increase the heart rate and oxygen intake
- To allow time for the teacher to mentally adjust the lesson plan to suit the attendees
- To introduce basic versions of moves or concepts to be used later in the class

You will notice that I have not listed stretching as an aim in the warm-up. Although we still see teachers stretching their students before class, it is generally considered to be unsafe to stretch before the body is fully warm. Advanced ballet dancers, gymnasts, and martial arts experts sometimes stretch to prepare the muscles, to avoid "ripping" the muscles during extreme moves. If you are teaching your students extreme moves in your belly dance classes, you may want to reconsider your lesson plan! Even professional ballet dancers do not need stretching before a belly dance class, because belly dance doesn't require the dancer to move outside her natural reach. Most of our students are not in that 0.1 percent of top athletes or dancers who may need to stretch their muscles before placing extreme demands on them – and these people generally have professionals keeping on top of the research for them. If you plan your lesson well and teach new moves later in the lesson when everyone has had a chance to fully warm up, then you shouldn't have any problems. If you want your dancers to be more flexible, the best way to help them is to repeat the basic moves regularly in class, which will gradually increase their range.

Warm up the body gently, taking into consideration the room temperature and your students' fitness levels as well as the kind of day they have already had. If you teach in a very hot country and your students have to climb four flights of stairs to get to your studio, you won't want to start with squats. If, however, your students have just walked through snow to come to your class and the heating isn't working, you would be better off allowing them to keep their coats on and to jog in place (or sending them home.)

Set the tone of your class and help everyone to relax by picking music that is soothing, gentle, and positive. Move with soft, flowing movements, and take time to talk to the group and perhaps introduce some of the ideas for that day's class. The joints are lubricated with synovial fluid, which protects them from wear and tear and acts as a shock absorber and cushion during movement. Distribute the synovial fluid by using gentle circling movements at each of the joints. I find it best to start at the bottom of the body and work up in order to not leave anything out. Watch as your students move to see if anyone is favoring one side of her body or pulling a face as she moves a joint. They may not be aware of any aches or pains until they start to move.

Once the body has been gently warmed up and the joints lubricated, then the warm-up can become more intense and upbeat. Pick music that is joyful and lighthearted with a regular beat throughout. Once your students know some belly dance moves, you can use them as part of your warm-up in a very relaxed, follow-me style.

Unless someone seems likely to injure herself, warm-up is not the time to correct any movements. Better that they bounce around and get everything warm than tense up and try to do a perfect hip drop. For new students, a simple step tap or walk in place is enough to warm the body. Add arms, hand moves, shoulder rolls, and changes in the size of the step to add variety and interest and to make sure the whole body is working. The body tends to glow – that is, sweat – once the muscles have reached a good working temperature, so take this as an indication that you have worked your students to the right level of intensity.

Practical Tip:

Before your first class, practice your warm-up every day for a week so that you don't run out of energy halfway through or sweat more than the students! Speaking while working out is so much harder than it looks and can mess with your natural breathing patterns. You want your students to feel like they've had a workout, maybe make them sweat a little, but you also need to be able to talk straight after your warm-up.

I find it helpful to have a basic move for each warm-up. That may be a step tap, step close step tap, march, or square walk. Mark your basic move with its own arm position and return to it often and before each change of arms or combination. This allows the students to return to the familiar if they got lost in the warm-up and to keep the same pattern as the rest of the class without feeling they look foolish. If you find someone is not keeping up or it looks like too much for them, call out and remind them that they can stick to the basic if they prefer. Continue with each change for at least a count of eight, if not sixteen or thirty-two. This allows the dancers to see what you are doing and get confident in their moves. If no one can do your warm-up, it is too hard. Warm-up time is not the best point to challenge your students mentally.

Think about your lesson when planning your warm-up. Focus on the parts of the body that will be working hard in the lesson, and introduce components that help with moves. It is wonderful to be able to say "You just did this in the warm-up" as you introduce a section of the main body of the lesson.

SUGGESTED WARM-UP FOR TOTAL BEGINNER DANCERS

With soft music, each move repeated around sixteen times:

Smile, nod, find your place in the room
Roll shoulders backward and forward
Heel and toe on each foot
Circle ankles, both ways, both feet
Circle knees, both ways, both sides
Draw a circle on the ground with the big toe, keeping the knee almost straight
   (this circles the hip joints)
Half hip rotation to the front
Half hip rotation to the back
Whole arm backward (backstroke)
Whole arm forward (crawl stroke)
Wrist circles, both ways, both sides
Piano fingers
Look over one shoulder, hold, look over other shoulder, hold, repeat
Gentle shake of the whole body

With upbeat music, each move repeated around sixteen times:

Step tap right and left (basic)
Add a sweep of arms down and across the body
Make the sweep large
Back to basic
Sweep the arms over the top of the head
Make the sweep small and dancelike
Back to basic
Shoulder roll in direction of step
Arms in front to make shoulder roll dancelike
Back to basic
Step and point toe in front
Bring opposite arm in front too
Back to basic
Step and point toe behind
Bring arms above head
Bring down same arm as foot behind
Back to basic
Bring shoulders forward and
    back (slow shoulder shim-
    my)
Back to basic
Big step to side, tap
Back to basic
Tiny step to side, tap
Finish

SUGGESTED WARM-UP FOR EXPERIENCED DANCERS

With soft music, each move repeated around sixteen times:

Smile, nod, find your place in the room
Roll shoulders backward and forward (right, left, right, right, left, right, left, left)
Heel and toe on each foot
Circle ankles, both ways, both feet
Circle knees, both ways, both sides
Draw a circle on the ground with the big toe, keeping the knee almost straight (this circles the hip joints): three times on one side, step close, repeat on the other side
Half hip rotation to the front with a small shimmy
Half hip rotation to the back, lowering the chest with a straight back, bend knees, unroll up to standing
Whole arm backward (backstroke) with tummy pulses
Whole arm forward (crawl stroke) with knee bounce
Wrist circles, both ways, both sides over snake arms
Piano fingers over "paint the fence" forward arms
Look over one shoulder, look over other shoulder, repeat
Gentle shake of the whole body

With upbeat music, each move repeated around sixteen times:

Vine step (basic)
Add inward circle arms (like polishing the mirror)
Back to basic
Add outward circle arms
Back to basic
Add on shoulder roll patterns (right, left, right, right, left, right, left, left)
Back to basic
Add a gentle shimmy
Add an arm frame (fingers to eyebrows)
Back to basic
Add a hip lift on each step
Add an arm frame (arms out in a W)
Back to basic
Swing hips side to side with each step
Add moving arms (falling leaf)
Back to basic
Add an extra-large shimmy
Back to basic
Hip lifts on a vine to the right, shimmy over a vine to the left
Add arms
Back to basics
Finish

TEACHING BASIC MOVES

You are already an experienced belly dancer, and this is not a book about new moves, but I would like to explain how I teach the moves that I cover in my beginners level classes. You may focus your beginners classes in a different direction, one that is right for you, but it is useful to make sure you understand how you are going to teach everything before you are on the spot. I have also noted any safety issues for each move to help prevent injuries.

When setting up a lesson plan, I cut and paste these reminders to make sure I cover each learning style during the lesson. I have used abbreviated notes in the list below; feel free to add your own thoughts and teach these moves in a way that suits your dance style and philosophy.

The following list includes examples of how to break down eleven basic moves for each of the learning styles. We have already covered the hip rotation and the maya in previous chapters.

Side to side/hip push/hip bump/sway/slide/tick tock
Show: Demonstrate move at different speeds and at different angles to the student.
Explain: Horizontal slide of hip that marks a beat
Story: Shutting the car door with your hip.
Count: 1, 2, 1, 2
Breakdown: Engaging your abs, slide hip straight out to each side in turn.
Why: Very basic way to mark a beat, folkloric, natural
Safety: Overstretching, overusing the knees
Make Physical Corrections

Figure eight/horizontal eight/backward eight/taqsim/snake hips
Show: Demonstrate move at different speeds and at different angles to the student.
Explain: Figure eight or infinity shape by hips done parallel to the floor
Story: Shape of a child's toy train track; sway like the wind
Count: 1, 2, 3, 4
Breakdown: Slide hips to a right front diagonal, take right hip back in a half circle, shift weight and hips to left, front diagonal, take left hip back in a half circle.
Why: Soft sway that fits to many melodies
Safety: Overstretching, overusing knees
Make Physical Corrections

Reverse figure eight/forward eight/reverse taqsim/jewel

Show: Demonstrate move at different speeds and at different angles to the student.

Explain: Figure eight or infinity shape by hips done parallel to the floor, same as figure eight but other direction

Story: It's the shape of a child's toy train track or feels more internal, wrapping a blanket around the hips.

Count: 1, 2, 3, 4

Breakdown: Slide hips to a back diagonal right, bring right hip forward in a half circle, shift weight and hips to a back, left diagonal, bring left hip forward in a half circle.

Why: Offers a very different mood from the other figure eight; gives dancers a chance to change direction while staying with the melody.

Safety: Overstretching, overusing knees

Make Physical Corrections

Hip lift/hip up/bump

Show: Demonstrate move at different speeds and at different angles to the student.

Explain: Hip moving straight up and returning to neutral

Story: Bouncing a toddler who is sitting on your hip.

Count: 1, 2, 1, 2/ up, and, up, and

Breakdown: Change posture to one foot, heel slightly lifted, in front, use abs and gluteus to bring hip up toward the rib cage, release abs and gluteus to have hip return to neutral position.

Why: Good to mark the beat, traditional in many styles

Safety: Using knees or ankles, twisting the move

Make Physical Corrections

Hip drop/hip down

Show: Demonstrate move at different speeds and at different angles to the student.

Explain: Hip moving down and returning to neutral

Story: Teenage girls with attitude who bounce their hip and look you up and down.

Count: 1, 2, 1, 2/ down, and, down, and

Breakdown: Change posture to one foot in front, check hips are still level. Relax muscles on side to drop, tense those muscles to bring the hip back to neutral.

Why: Good to mark a heavy beat, traditional in many styles

Safety: Overuse of knee, twisting the move, overstretching

Make Physical Corrections

Camel/undulation/Arabic/body wave
Show: Demonstrate move at different speeds and at different angles to the student.
Explain: A circle done by both hips that is parallel to the walls
Story: Imagine a bicycle wheel or a bridge and its reflection in the water.
Count: Varies
Breakdown: Starting with heavy hips in the center, move hips forward and up, then up and back, drop hips back and down, then forward and down, returning to the heavy hips position. Use abs and gluteus to power the move.
Why: Great workout for core, looks pretty from all angles, great travelling move
Safety: Back issues, overextending toward the back, going the other way and lifting through the back
Make Physical Corrections

Forward and back step/rocking horse/Turkish/scissors
Show: Demonstrate move at different speeds and at different angles to the student.
Explain: Basic footwork pattern
Story: Image that one foot is stuck to floor with gum and the other foot comes forward and back or visualize a marching soldier who can't decide where to go.
Count: 1,2,3,4/ Forward and back and
Breakdown: Right foot steps forward and left foot lifts from floor, left foot returns to the floor and right foot lifts, right foot steps back and left foot lifts, left foot returns to the floor and right foot lifts.
Why: Marks the beat, easy to layer over, traditional in many styles
Safety: Slipping
Make Physical Corrections

Shimmy
Show: Demonstrate move at different speeds and at different angles to the student.
Explain: Rapid movement of a part of the body
Story: Shake, vibrate
Count: Constant
Breakdown: On hips, use either a forward and back, up and down or side to side as a basic move. As move becomes smaller, it speeds up.
Why: traditional, audiences expect it, easy to layer over other moves
Safety: Tension, overuse of knees
Make Physical Corrections

Snake arms/arm rolls/ serpent waves/arm undulations

Show: Demonstrate move at different speeds and at different angles to the student.

Explain: Undulating move of the arms

Story: Painting a fence on either side of you or changing weights on old-fashioned scale.

Count: Varies

Breakdown: Lift right shoulder, right elbow, and right wrist, then flick fingers toward the ceiling while softening the wrist. Drop right shoulder, drop elbow, and drop wrist, then flick fingers toward the floor while softening the wrists. Repeat on the left. Drop on the right as you lift on the left.

Why: Classic belly dance move, easy to layer with other moves

Safety: Tension in shoulders, posture lost due to concentration

Make Physical Corrections

Single hip rotations/sideways circles/ Moroccan hip circle

Show: Demonstrate move at different speeds and at different angles to the student.

Explain: A circle done by one hip parallel to the wall

Story: Visualize one hip polishing the wall, bicycle wheel.

Count: Varies

Breakdown: From the foot-in-front posture, drop the hip down as in a hip drop. Move the hip up and forward into the forward position of a hip twist. Move the hip up and back to neutral as if in a hip lifted position, then back and down slightly behind the line of the hip. Finally, move the hip down and forward to the starting position.

Why: Single hip move to follow the melody, looks good at various angles

Safety: Twisting hip out of line, overstretching

Make Physical Corrections

Three-quarter shimmy/Egyptian walk/hagala/Algerian

Show: Demonstrate move at different speeds and at different angles to the student.

Explain: A way to use the popular 3/4 beat in which three things happen over a count of four.

Story: Walking like you want someone to notice you.

Count: 1, 2, 3, and? Down, side, up, pause

Breakdown: Take a step onto your right foot and drop the hip. With your weight shifting, push your right hip to the right. Lift your left foot and your left hip. Pause. Repeat by stepping onto your left foot with a drop, sliding your left hip to the left, lifting your right foot and hip, and pausing.

Why: Introduction to other three-quarter walks and shimmies

Safety: Overstretching, slipping

Make Physical Corrections

This is by no means a comprehensive list of moves, but I am sure you have the idea by now. When setting up your lesson plans, take the time to be sure that you are ready and prepared to teach each move and combination for all learning styles.

Finally, I should admit that I do find teaching the basic moves occasionally repetitive and perhaps even a little boring. I cannot imagine how many times over the years I have taught someone to hip drop, but it must be in the thousands. What keeps it fresh and enjoyable for me is to see how the move works on each body, to enjoy the "lightbulb" moment when the move fits and feels fantastic to the dancer, and to challenge myself to teach the moves clearly and in a way that suits each student.

For most of your students, these early classes will be the foundation of their learning, and the longer you can spend on helping them perfect their basic moves, the stronger they will become as dancers. It is always more exciting to teach new moves or concepts you are dealing with in your own practice, but do not force those topics on your beginner students when really they need to be perfecting their basics. If you can, try to teach a beginners class followed by something more advanced; that way you can have an outlet for your creativity, without risking your baby dancers' moving too fast.

I also ask my more advanced dancers to continue with a beginner level class as a way to drill their core moves and to focus on the dance form beyond the new topic or performance piece. Not only do they get a workout and time to focus on perfecting their technique, but these experienced dancers also act as a bridge, motivating the new students to move onward and upward. Try to discount multiple classes so that money does not become an obstacle to those who want to move from recreational student into more serious study.

In belly dance we never grow out of our basic moves; we may layer, shimmy, turn, and pose, but a good figure eight remains at the very core of our dance. Allow your dancers the time and space to attempt perfection.

THAT TA-DAH! MOMENT

The Ta-dah! moment could be described as the main point of the lesson, or the payoff for learning moves or drilling them. It can be the goal, the culmination, or just an excuse to have fun with a new skill set.

Sometimes the lesson is planned around the Ta-dah!; other times the Ta-dah! is planned to round off the lesson. Both are effective.

For example, if the goal of the lesson is to learn a new combination that will fit into a choreography, then the lesson might focus on drilling each move, adding in layers to moves like arms or shimmies, or perhaps trying the floor pattern with more basic moves. Once the students have each ingredient for the combination, they can put them together in the Ta-dah! section, where they learn the combination.

Or perhaps you have noticed that your students have become sloppy with their hip rotations and you want to focus on getting them perfect. You can spend some time talking about hip rotation problems, mixing large and small rotations and getting the students to focus on perfection, either on their own moves in a mirror or working with a partner. After all that hard work, you can plan some circle time (everyone stands in a circle and faces inward) as your Ta-dah! They could try to keep their rotations perfect and unbroken while you call out layers, like "Snake arms," "Travel to the left," "Shoulder rolls," "Chest circles," or "Sing the lyrics." Or you could get out some flash cards with basic moves on them. Ask the dancers to perform the move you have called for a count of eight or four and then return to their basic move, which in this example is the hip rotation, without breaking the flow. This would help them with both recognizing the names of the moves and linking the moves together in a flowing manner.

Ta-dah! moments need to be lighthearted and upbeat. They are a payoff for working hard in the lesson, both physically and mentally. They help the dancer to understand why we work hard and stay focused: by drilling the combination thirty times, we can now use it as the chorus to this track; by perfecting this move, we can now layer it with a tummy roll; by shimmying with our arms out and lifted, we can now do a super cool barrel turn without the arms flying everywhere.

We want the students to see how much they have learned and how useful their skills are to them as dancers. This is not a time for correction (unless they are moving in an unsafe way), but rather for celebration.

When planning your Ta-dah! moments, find a balance between using the familiar and the new. If the class stood in a circle last week and took turns suggesting a move to dance to for the next eight counts, try splitting the class up into small groups for this week's class but have them do the same kind of thing. Each member of the group gets to pick a move, and they dance each move in turn. If you have a more advanced group, they may want to get creative and mix up the counts.

For example, your beginner subgroup might do:

Eight hip circles
Eight hip drops
Eight shimmies
Eight figure eights
And repeat

While your more advanced group might do:

Two hip drops and a shimmy
Two hip drops and a shimmy
Four figure eights
Four reverse figure eights
Four figure eights
Four reverse figure eights
And repeat

If you have split your class into groups, allow enough time for each group to either show off to the others or get positive feedback in front of the whole class; for example:

"So our new ladies did a great job of keeping it simple. Their hip rotations were perfect, and we had some creative arm frames going on, which looked lovely. Over in the corner, this group was really interpreting the music, listening for changes, and adapting their combination to fit. Great job, everyone."

Sometimes you will have an amazing idea for a Ta-dah! moment and find that you want to spend almost the whole of your lesson on it. That is totally fine, but perhaps keep some time in the beginning to reinforce part of last week's class or to build a sweat. Students may not be happy if they just talked all lesson, even if they learned about all the instruments in the Egyptian orchestra in that hour. It would be better to use the same Ta-dah! idea for three or four weeks in a row. For example you could split the instruments into subsections (wind, string, percussion) and each week teach a couple of combinations that work well with music that highlights those instruments in your Ta-dah!

For week one you might focus on figure eight shapes on different parts of the body during the technique section of your class and then let them flow between chest, shoulder, and hip eights in time to a beautiful nay taqsim as their Ta-dah!

The next week could focus on small hip shimmies, tummy flutters, and shoulder shimmies working toward a Ta-dah! of a guitar taqsim.

The third lesson can highlight heavy hits and steps to drumbeats, leading to a Ta-dah! of anticipating drum patterns in a drum solo.

For the last week you can divide your class into groups of three and ask each dancer to dance to only one instrument. Among the three of them they can express all the complex layers of a belly dance classic and discuss which instrument is the most important during each section of the music.

Room formation will play an important role in how your Ta-dah! will work, as I discussed previously. But be aware of how exposed or safe each dancer feels in expressing her creativity. Circles allow each dancer to see everyone but can also increase the fear of making a mistake. Use circles when you are confident all group members understand the rules of the game and will be working easily within their own abilities. Subgroups allow more privacy but also hide the students away from your line of sight or hearing. Make sure all know that their opinions count, and place strong personalities away from the more nervous. Extrovert dancers will love the chance to dance in the center of a circle and show off the move they have just mastered. More introverted dancers might like time in their subgroup to see how it works with other moves and where it fits into a combination before performing it to the other subgroups at the end of the session.

When planning your Ta-dah! here are a few things to consider:

- Is it fun?
- Does it fit with the goal of the class?
- Does it help a skill set develop?
- Does it help with a problem area?
- Does it reinforce other parts of the lesson?
- Does it fit in with the tone of the term?
- Is it too complex?
- Will it fit within the time?

- Does it have something for everyone?
- Is it easy to explain?
- Is it creative?
- How will you split your group?
- What formation will work best?
- How is it similar to last week's Ta-dah! moment?
- What worked previously?
- What does the class like to do?
- Do you have fun music that works?
- How can you make it more of a game?

COOL COOLDOWNS

Your cooldown section has a number of aims:

- To mark the end of the lesson
- To give the teacher time to remind students of all they have learned
- To relax the students
- To bring the heart rate down to normal
- To give the students time to check their body for injury or tension
- To regulate breathing
- To ease the body with gentle stretching
- To change the tone and prepare dancers to exit the dance space

Cooldown time needs to focus on both the body's needs and the needs of the student's mind. Very often the dancers have shut out worries or stresses from their everyday lives in order to be fully in the moment while dancing. Taking time in the cooldown to breathe and relax allows the brain to file away belly dance information and avoid adding it to the dancer's stress list. The body also needs time to return to its comfortable levels. Take longer over your cooldowns if your students have worked hard and built up a sweat. Look at them to check that their flushed cheeks and rapid breathing are returning to normal.

The cooldown is also a way to mark the end of your lesson. Some teachers like to turn the end of their cooldown into a small ceremony, perhaps by bringing their hands together and repeating a saying, expressing gratitude to the students with a round of applause, or taking everyone's hands in a circle and practicing deep breathing together. Find a way to end your lesson that suits your teaching style and that is more purposeful than simply turning off the music and shutting off the lights.

This list works for students at beginner levels upwards, simply add more belly dance moves as students learn them:

Pace on the spot or walk the room at a medium tempo.

Continue to walk, but place both hands on one hip and look over the opposite shoulder. Hold for a count of eight. Repeat to the other side. Repeat but hold for four. Repeat. Repeat but hold for two. Repeat about a dozen more times.

Walk while rolling the shoulders.

Mix single shoulder rolls forward with double shoulder rolls backward.

Walk at half tempo with a big push to the side of the hips.

Continue with the big swing of the hips but add matching arms.

Stand on one spot and reach one arm above the head, straight up, then across the body, then down to the floor, and finally reaching out in front of the body. Repeat with the other arm.

Bring hands to the tummy and relax the shoulders.

Invite students to close their eyes, if they wish, and to breathe deeply.

Mention each body part and ask that students check their posture and also relax and unknot any tension.

List the work covered in that lesson, using positive wording.

Invite each dancer to take time to thank her body for all its hard work and to take another deep breath.

Allow the students to drop their arms and shake out their hands.

Thank them for coming to class and making your lesson so enjoyable for you.

Applaud them and take a bow.

With more advanced lessons and students, you may need to adjust your cooldown to allow stretching of muscles that you have used in that lesson. For example, if they all have been dancing on their toes, you may want to have them stretch out their calves. Use your own body as a judge of what muscle groups you have used that need additional stretching, or ask the students. Do not overextend, bounce, or put weight behind a stretch. Instead, find a pose that is comfortable or slightly uncomfortable and hold that pose for a count of eight or for thirty seconds. Repeat a couple of times on each side. Always check in your waiver whether your students have any injuries that mean they need a doctor's approval of suitable stretches, and allow your students time and space to practice stretches their doctors may have suggested.

These are the stretches that I use occasionally:

Calf stretch

To stretch out the back of the lower leg. Place one leg half a step behind the other with both heels down and both knees soft. Bend the front knee forward and bring the hips forward while keeping the back straight. This stretches the leg that is behind.

Hamstring stretch

To stretch out the back of the upper leg. Keeping the back straight, lean forward and let the arms hang down toward the floor. If the dancers can touch the floor, encourage them to walk their hands back toward their feet, but to maintain the straight back. To end this stretch, bend the knees, tuck the pelvis, and roll up slowly. Lifting the head too quickly can cause dizziness.

Quad stretch

The quadriceps run along the front of the upper leg. Using a partner for balance, lift the foot up toward the bottom, keeping the knees together, and hold the ankle. Soften the supporting leg and hold the abs tight to help with balance. Students may need to hold the bottom hem of their pant leg if they can't reach the ankle.

Shoulder stretch

This stretch is for the back of the shoulders. Bring one arm across the body and hold it close to the chest with the other arm; hold. Repeat on the other side.

Neck stretch

Lean your head to the right side and slightly toward the front. Keep your shoulders down but bring your right hand up and drape it over the top of your head. There is no need to pull your head down. Repeat on the other side.

Upper back stretch

Stand with good posture and bring your arms in front of your body at about shoulder level. Hold. Bring the arms back, bending at the elbows. Hold and repeat.

Attitudes about stretching change all the time. Some believe it to be outmoded and unlikely to be of much benefit for all but the elite athletes. An alternative way to train muscles or to "elongate" them is to repeat the desired exercise in a soft way, regularly. It could therefore be suggested that the best way to stretch out after learning a figure eight would be some gentle figure eights.

It is worth checking with any students who have had a recent injury whether they have been assigned any specific stretches by their doctor and allow them time to repeat those stretches during your class time.

Some people believe that stretching will help prevent injury or muscle aches, help them to react faster or make their muscles stronger. Others don't believe any of this. You will be likely to meet people from both camps while teaching dance.

If stretching may not help prevent injury or aches and doesn't make us a better dancer, why do it? First, stretching does feel good. Just as we might like to have a little stretch in the morning before we get out of bed, so it is nice to stretch out a bit before we put on our coat and walk home. Second, many dancers expect to do stretching in class. If you don't do any stretching, your students may feel that you don't know what you are doing or that they have been cheated out of an important part of the lesson. Finally, at any time in life stretches do help people to pay attention to their bodies. They may follow a stretch with a little self-massage or allow their mind to notice a sore shoulder from too much gardening. Keep up-to-date with modern stretching technique and thinking, and remember to always be gentle with your students.

TEACHING DANCERS TO SMILE

When we list all the things that we want our students to be able to master, it's hard to prioritize that into a short course. Maybe they should be learning finger cymbals from week one? Drum solos or veils? Three-quarter shimmy or walking shimmy? Which is more important and should be taught first?

As the class teacher, you get to plan your course to focus on what you think is most important and to start your students off in the direction you would like them to take to become a great dancer. Personally, I think that smiling needs to be pretty high up on that list. It's something almost everyone can already do, but somehow the smile disappears before half of all belly dancers step onto the stage. My students know that I will forgive them almost any technique mistake in a performance, just so long as they engage with the audience and smile.

The first thing you can do is smile a lot yourself. Show your students just how much you love to dance by allowing your face to light up. Second, remind them to smile as they learn each move. It can be natural to frown or bite the lip as we concentrate, but encourage them to think of their smile as part of their basic posture. Finally, take time to break down how to smile and include this when talking about layering moves. Discuss the importance of a natural smile that reaches the eyes, and practice smiles in front of a mirror and to classmates.

Belly dance students often want to look moody, but if you watch even the darkest of performers they always have a hint of a smile. You will have students who hate their smile or who complain, but it needs to be drilled and practiced just like any other move.

Maintaining a full, beaming smile for a whole performance can be difficult (and slightly scary for the audience), so get your dancers to practice turning it up at regular intervals, perhaps with each change of move or angle to the audience.

Please populate the belly dance world with joyful, smiling belly dancers for me to enjoy during my retirement.

TEACHING DANCERS TO EXPRESS EMOTION

Belly dance has such a wonderful emotional side to it, which attracts many of us to this dance form above others. We talk to our students about feeling the music and letting it move us, but sometimes those kinds of expressions don't connect with the dancers and are not reflected in their performances.

Start in the early days of lessons by showing your own emotions and taking every opportunity to show how you connect to the music. Tell not only the stories behind the lyrics, but also how each piece has touched your life. Shimmy to your first solo; dance with a veil to the music your son can play on flute.

When I first started dancing there was a classmate who really inspired me. She was tall, graceful, and majestic. At her funeral they played a very popular piece of music that she had used for one of the first performances I had seen. Even fifteen years later, I still play that music for my students during their first ten-week course. It reminds me of how gracefully she turned and twirled her veil, as if she was floating an inch off the ground. Sometimes I tell my students about her; other times I just say that this is really special music for me. I hope that they can see something of her influence in the way I dance.

Dancing with emotion takes practice, just as much as being able to turn or shimmy. Ask your students if they like your music choices and how it makes them feel. Focus on the idea that we are all human, with common stories. So many songs are about "the man that she loves too much" or "he promises to be good if only she would take him back," "the end of love," or "her captivating eyes." For many of us these songs bring back memories of past relationships, mis-

takes we made, or the lovers who shone light into our lives. Be gentle with your students; there may be some who are in a bad place, who use belly dance class as a way to take time off, but equally they may appreciate the emotional release dance can bring. Keep your comments very light, but allow the students time to express their connections through dance. It takes only a moment to introduce a piece of music with a key lyric or an outline of its general feeling.

Use familiar music to help the dancers practice emotional dance. Each of us connects to different types of music, but popular music is generally very popular with most people, and even if a student doesn't like your music choice, she may find it easier to understand the emotion you want the class to portray.

Pick out a favorite, upbeat holiday tune and ask your students about how they feel at the approach of the holiday season. Do they dread the family visits, arguments, and sharing their homes? Or do they remember the anticipation from their childhood? Or perhaps they love the excitement of shopping for food or gifts.

Film sound tracks can be a great source of inspiring emotional music. If you hear something on the radio that makes you feel tearful, make a note of the name of the song or piece. Once your students have made a connection with some music, try to find something more Arabic or Turkish that evokes the same kind of feelings for you. Let them see that emotions are universal and musicians are particularly skillful at tapping into our feelings.

I prefer to run a whole course or a long workshop on emotion in dance, working with more advanced dancers who don't feel the need for a new move in each lesson. I am happy to have them share their own selection of music, and I ask them to explain the stories behind the songs and how it makes them feel. You can explore body language and how we show fear, sadness, joy, and love in basic dance moves and arm positioning. Take the time to watch each of them dance, and give them feedback on what parts of the story you could see and what needed more attention. Try to pick out music that fits more into your style of belly dance but that has a story or feeling similar to that of the music your students selected. Remind them of how they showed those emotions before, and ask them to find that same connection.

Emotion, like body language and facial expressions, is extremely hard to fake. The audience is not fooled by the false smile or the finger pointing to the heart. Teach your students to be brave, research their music, and find a story that means something to them. They will reward you with honest, emotional performances.

THE EYES HAVE IT

Once your dancers are smiling and expressing emotion in their dance, it is time to give them an outlet for all that energy and thought behind their facial expressions. I talk about the tripod of focus as an introduction to stagecraft: three points at which to aim the eyes and the different feelings they express. Sometimes it's easier to explain these eye positions as the self, the audience, and the other.

The self

As part of the charm of belly dance, we are allowed to look with wonder at the many amazing things we can make our own body do. For some of us, there are parts of the body we can't see while still maintaining good posture. My bust blocks my view of my hips, but no one in the audience needs to know that when I look downward to admire my hip drops. Sometimes we have to fake it – looking over our shoulder as if we could see a hip shimmy, dropping our eyes as if we could see our tummy roll – but still that eye focus is on ourselves. We also use our arms to lead the eyes to where the action is or just watch a beautiful wrist roll. When we focus on ourselves, we look internally, like we are daydreaming. Our emotions look introverted, be they happiness or sadness. This is how we "dance as if no one is watching," and it's very beautiful to watch. But it also excludes the audience and can make them feel voyeuristic or unwelcome. This is why our second focus is . . .

Our audience

It may seem obvious, but dancers need to be aware of their audience and dance to them. If you have small children at your feet, you will need to look down to make eye contact with them. If you have a full theater with audience in the upper balcony, then you need to lift your chin and smile up to them as well. Sometimes a restaurant may clear some room for the dancer with a dozen tables in front but still one or two behind, and those need some attention too.

Be aware of how the dancer's face and look changes as she looks around her audience. Looking downward can look flirty or shy; looking upward can look proud or arrogant. In contrast, gazing directly at the audience makes the dancer look extroverted and engaged. Encourage your dancers to look around and to make eye contact with the audience, even if they can't actually see them in the darkness. Making eye contact is something that many of us find difficult. Again, lead by example and give your dancers the chance to be both performer and audience in lesson time. When I can't see the audience, I like to imagine children sitting in the front row, dazzled by the sequins and swept away with the fantasy. In the middle rows I put my classmates and fellow dancers, who are encouraging but also want to see my skills. Away up in the balcony I put my parents and my teachers, those who have encouraged me over the years and want to see me succeed. Dancing to the audience makes them feel included and part of the dance. Just keep in mind that focusing on them for too long can be overpowering for the audience and may make them feel as if you are disconnected from your own dancing.

The other

Finally, many belly dancers dance for a higher reason. From the fabulous hippie dancers and the deeply religious to the scientists and the athletes (and all the other shades and combinations), belly dance offers something "other" that they connect to. We see a wonderful, joyous expression cross the dancer's face, usually accompanied by an upward glance. Perhaps it is thankfulness for having found in belly dance an outlet for the happiness they have in their life.

This may be the hardest eye position to teach, but start by allowing it to happen naturally. I begin with that image of our teachers up in the rafters of a theater looking down on us dancers and wishing us well. Dancers will find their own route to replacing those teachers with images that mean something in their life.

From this tripod of focus – ourselves, our audience, and our other – we can layer on other positions, a full clock face of directions in which to aim the head. But always give your students a reason for their eye and face positions. Keep it logical and try to spend approximately one third of the time on each focus for a well-rounded performance.

From eye positions you can move on to chin positions and chest and hip angles so that they become aware of how the whole body looks to their audience, no matter where they are sitting, and their dancing becomes more complex.

TEACHING TURNS

There are a few reasons why students struggle with turns. First, they just don't get it; second, they are hard to explain; and third, they take an unusual mix of effort and skill.

We may find turns hard to explain because many of us teachers have been adding turns to our dances ever since we did our baby ballet classes, so we really can't remember a time when turns didn't just happen. If you have a problem in your teaching, it helps to think about how you would teach something that you personally would find hard to do.

For example, a dance turn is not unlike a gymnastic or parkour vault in the way energy and effort are transferred at high speed. To vault over a wall, you need to run toward it, place the hands in exactly the right position, and transfer the forward movement of the run into getting your hips over the wall while using upper body strength to lift you up and over. Keep the head up and get the feet down, land on both feet at the same time, and soften the impact into your knees. No problem! You are now ready to vault – right?

Take a moment to think about everything that you fear when I suggest you go out and vault over a wall. (If vaults are easy for you, how about imagining having to skydive, or to surgically remove an ingrown toenail). I fear that I will run straight into the wall, that my arms will give out, that I won't make it over, or that I will fall on the other side. Although I have seen other people vault a wall, I don't really understand how they do it, I don't trust my body strength, and I fear looking foolish and hurting myself. The thing with vaults (and turns, and cartwheels, and every other untried skill we doubt we can master) is that those doubts are at least 50 percent of the problem. Just to begin a vault, we have to run at that wall with confidence and attack. The fear and doubt kills the attack before the vault is even started, and so begins a pattern of failure that leads to a belief that vaults are only for superheroes and not for slightly overweight middle-aged ladies like myself. Watch your students as you introduce them to turns; you will see those same fears written on their faces.

When teaching turns, allow generous time to work on the foot patterns, the arm work, and where that extra energy is being built and transferred. Let's look at a 360 degree pivot turn:

> Take half a step forward with your right foot
> Lift up onto the balls of both feet
> Pivot on the balls to your left, so you face the back of the room (180 degrees)
> The right foot is now behind the body, the left in front.
> Step forward on your right foot again
> Lift onto the balls of both feet again
> Pivot on the balls to the left again to complete the turn (360 degrees)

Practice this turn a few times, keeping your focus on your feet. You will notice how stiff it feels and that it has no flow. The foot technique is correct, but this is not how a dancer does it and builds it into a fast, pretty turn. What happens with your hip as you pivot this turn faster? Is it a hip lift or a hip bump, or simply a strong weight shift that adds momentum to the turn? Now think about the shoulders. See how they add to the power behind the movement. When I pivot turn, I lift the chest slightly on the right as I step forward and do a very tiny shoulder roll on the right, which is echoed with a left-sided chest lift and shoulder roll as I pivot. As the rest of the body joins in, the power behind the turn increases and the speed and smoothness of the turn improves.

If you try to teach this chest lift and shoulder roll technique to beginner dancers, you will confuse them and add in too many layers for them to focus on. Instead, focus on allowing their body to find its own power to put behind the turn.

Once your dancers have the footwork down, work on just that first step and how you can put energy behind it by stepping with purpose. Get them to add a 90-degree turn in their upper body as they push the weight forward in the first step and by using extra energy from the hip. As they repeat that step forward with energy, they will find themselves having to put the brakes on to stop the turn from continuing. A dozen or so repeats and they are starting to put more effort into halting the turn than the startup power. At this point it feels more logical to take that pivot on to 180 degrees, and they are not dizzy or confused from too many turns, but they can understand how throwing themselves into committing to the turn is going to help make it happen.

This same theory works with walk-through turns, barrel turns, and pirouettes; work out where your energy is going to come from and how to put the maximum energy into the first part of the turn. For a barrel turn, I have my student practice "pick a penny" where they place the foot forward at the same time as they reach for a penny on the floor with the arm on the same side as the foot, while still keeping nice lines and good posture. Once they are confident in that step forward, you can add in a preparation of a step back and a 90-degree turn of the upper body. This preparation plus the "pick a penny" has already turned the upper body 180 degrees, built energy, reinforced the complex arm positions, and increased the dancer's confidence in being able to complete the turn – and again, no one is dizzy.

Posture and centering are the key to balanced turns, and students feel happier if they know their start points and finish points. Spotting looks nice and helps with dizziness but may be one too many layers to add on in the early days. Save it for the second week. If your students can't spot, let them focus on their hand as they turn, but encourage them to blur out the rest of their surroundings so as to stave off dizziness. A quick heel bounce at the end of a turn can help stop the ear fluids from moving and greatly reduce dizziness.

Great turning takes practice every day, so it is not enough to drill in a weekly class. If it's something you love and want to share with your students, encourage them to practice and slowly build up how much they do in each lesson.

Give your students the chance to watch you turn and then try to repeat that turn at half time. Break it down and add a count, even if the count is one-pre-pare, two-turn. Sort the group into pairs so that one dancer can turn while the other acts as her spotter, keeping her safe in the room and looking for the upright posture and centering of the turn. Finally, try not to open your choreographies with too many turns, or you students may feel confused and off center from the start.

ACROSS THE FLOOR

You may remember across the floor from your early ballet lessons. It never goes out of fashion and is a popular way to reinforce moves, encourage creativity, and change your class formation. At its simplest, the teacher starts a line of students at one side of the room; she travels the room doing a move, and everyone else follows. The main reason for going diagonally across the room is to have farther to travel. It is best to give each dancer a slight head start on the next to allow for variations in speed and step size. Once a dancer has made it across the floor, she walks around the edge of the room and rejoins the back of the line to wait her turn again.

Across the floor allows space to travel and link moves together, while also giving students time to see how the moves look on different bodies and other students' styling choices. As teachers we can step out of the line and watch each dancer in turn as she travels, looking for good posture along with the desired execution of the move or combination.

Here are a few ways to use across the floor in your class setting:

- **Simple drill.** A travelling move, like a travelling hip lift.
- **Adding arm layers.** Drill a basic move, and on each "lap," change the arms: hip lifts with tribal styling; arms open with a matching wrist turn; arms low to frame each lift; one arm out, the other in the hair.
- **Creative drum work.** A shimmy layered walk with hits highlighting the music (shimmy, shimmy, shimmy, hips, chest, hips).
- **Creative combinations.** Start with a basic travelling move and cross the floor once. Ask the next person in the line to add a move. Cross the floor with your move repeated four times and the new move four times. Ask the next person to add a move – and so on. As the teacher you may have to adapt their moves to fit the music or to allow a return to the leading leg, but these combinations usually work beautifully.

Asking your students to move across the floor helps you to watch them for longer and to see which of them are comfortable using strong frames or interesting arm layers, who counts as she dances, who has an animated face, and so on.

FREE DANCING/IMPROVISING

Free dancing or improvisation is the very soul of belly dance. I remember being told in a class to "Dance! Don't think, dance!"

As a teacher you must facilitate that wonderful moment when the body understands the music and the movements expected of it, and the dance weeps from the pores as naturally as sweat while the dancer dissolves into the music.

Some students will come to class already prepared to improvise to music, but most won't, and it is our hard task to guide them through the baby steps necessary to reach a skill and confidence level that will make it work for them. If you introduce free dance too early, you may face a roomful of students unwilling to dance at all. Too late, and they may have become so used to dancing behind you that they can't move unless you do.

I think the secret of introducing improvisation is to do so in small doses and without presenting it as improvising.

The first task is to have the students dance without their simply following your bouncing bum. After each setup and demonstration, move around the room, making corrections and planting the idea that they can continue dancing without you standing in front of them.

This same problem is solved with across the floor work or splitting the groups into duets and trios to dance together. They can no longer see you and are therefore already dancing without you.

Next, introduce the idea that they are good at hearing the layers in the music and already know which moves work. Describe moves as "soft" or "melodic" and "sharp" or "hits," and play music with a clear melody or regular beat, mixed so the moves are easily heard. Play a simple tune and ask the dancers to switch between one soft move and one sharp as they hear the changes in the music. It's important to emphasize that there is no right or wrong way to interpret music, and if you can hear it and you can show it, you are right.

Focus on the difference between drilling a move and using it to dance with. As belly dancers we break almost as many rules as we make: dancing half a figure eight and staying there to shoulder shimmy; dropping four times to our right and only twice, but slower, to the left. Our preparation moves are almost as varied as our recognized moves, and when the music stops, we may stop or sometimes we may allow our breathing to replace the music. During drills and practice, it's important to do the moves perfectly, but during improvisation the imperfections add an extra seasoning to the flavor of our dance.

I like to play my students a piece of nay or violin taqsim and ask them to unwind like a ball of wool: circles within circles, changes of direction, angle, speed, and size. This helps them to visualize the music and see their moves as part of it.

Help them become familiar with the key phrases, drum patterns, and popular songs in your style of belly dance. Middle Eastern and belly dance music can seem unpredictable at first, but the more we hear, the more we recognize recurring patterns. Allow your students time to absorb the feel of your music choices. Pick out highlights over the weeks by selecting music that repeats a drum pattern or with a fast pace that drops to a beautiful taqsim.

Structured improvisation holds the dancer to a framework while allowing her to express her creativity and personality. Set up a chorus or opening section for the students to improvise to, but provide them with some structure; for example:

> *"Travel during the opening four phrases and then do something simple with still, framing arms so the audience can really see you. Hit the first four beats softly and pause, but when they repeat, hit them harder, so as to contrast with the next phrase, which is a violin. You may want to move your shoulders or chest, then repeat the hard hits, violin, hard hits, violin, and then shimmy."*

You have told the students what to expect and how to dance, but not forced your style or favorite moves on them.

Finally, make sure you improvise from time to time and perform improvisation for them to enjoy, either in a performance setting or simply while they are dancing too. Show how much you enjoy losing yourself in the music and how beautiful that can be for an audience to share.

SPATIAL AWARENESS

As performing belly dancers it is easier for us to visualize a stage and audience or a busy restaurant than it is for our students. Being able to picture different dance settings helps to animate the dancer's face and prepare her for future performances. Dancers who dance only in front of a mirror tend to reflect that in a performance setting, with their eyes set to the middle distance and hip height. Mirrors are a wonderful teaching aid, giving your students a better view of you as you teach and helping them to see their skills evolve, but you should take every opportunity to move them away from the safety of the mirrors and toward the other walls of your dance space. Cross the floor and improvise out of sight of any mirrors if you can, so that the dancers focus on their own bodies and gain an inner confidence in how their dancing looks to an audience. After teaching a combination or choreography, split up the group so that the dancers understand how it looks from the outside as well as how it feels to dance with eyes watching you.

To be a great dancer you need to also be a great audience member, so encourage your students to watch dance as well as perform. Attend hafla, stage shows, and restaurant shows to encourage learning from the strengths and weaknesses of others. Teach your students to critique rather than criticize performances, learning how to improve their work rather than feeling enhanced by others' mistakes. Don't let your students critique in the performance space or offer their thoughts to the performers.

With more advanced dancers you can play with the relationship between performer and audience with experiments of distance between the dancer and the audience. Ask them to sit at the performer's feet or in a chair just a few feet away or watch from across the room. How does the relationship change? How close is too close?

As dancers we have a huge space to explore. Some people find 3D thinking really hard and can't imagine how their body moves through the space they use. Start in the very early days by defining the three major planes of your room: the height, the width, and the depth. When you jump or look up and down, you are exploring the height. When you walk toward and away from the mirror, you are exploring the depth, and when you face the mirror and open your arms, you are exploring the width.

Practical Tip:
Explore these directions with your chest. The chest rises and falls through the height; it moves forward and back through the depth and from side to side along the width.

You can use the idea of "being parallel" as a more visual way to define these spaces:

- A chest circle can be parallel with the mirror in the same way that, when cleaning the mirror, you would make a circle with your hand.
- A chest circle can be parallel with the floor, like an LP on a turntable.
- A chest circle can be parallel with the walls, like a bicycle wheel turning (this is sometimes called a chest camel).

It is possible to use your room to create even more points of reference in your practice and performance space. It is easiest to do this by naming your walls; some studios paint the walls different colors to help with that process. Usually our front wall, which will become the audience, is a mirror in the studio. The back wall often has a clock, so that the teacher can keep an eye on the time while facing her students (most dance teachers learn to read a clock in mirror image). Let us then imagine that one side wall has windows and the other has a painting. For brevity, I am going to name each wall after its focal point: mirror, clock, window, painting. Practice this in your current space.

You can point your hand to the following areas of your room:

- Mirror center
- Clock wall center
- Painting wall center
- Window wall center
- Mirror wall meets window wall
- Mirror meets painting
- Clock meets window
- Clock meets painting
- Mirror wall meets floor
- Window meets floor
- Painting meets floor
- Clock meets floor
- Mirror wall meets ceiling
- Window meets ceiling
- Painting meets ceiling
- Clock meets ceiling
- Mirror wall meets painting wall meets floor
- Mirror meets painting meets ceiling
- Mirror meets window meets floor
- Mirror meets window meets ceiling
- Clock meets painting meets floor
- Clock meets painting meets ceiling
- Clock meets window meets floor
- Clock meets window meets ceiling

You have pointed to the center of the walls, the corners of the room, the top edges, and the bottom edges.

Some artists prefer to describe the space using other terms, like stage directions or right and left, but the theory remains the same and opens up the opportunity for the teacher to use the space to better describe what she wants; for example:

"One hand is pointing to the center of the wall with the window. The other hand points to the middle of the mirror. Step toward the mirror and push the hip toward the window. On the hit, glance down to the floor where the mirror meets the blue wall, then look back at the audience as you step back."

"Face the mirror to window diagonal; bring the hand up to point to the same diagonal. Take the arm across past the mirror and to the mirror to fire exit corner, leaning the head so you can follow the hand, but not moving the body. Bring the hand and eyes down to the hip. Two hip drops and then move the eyes to very center of the mirror and smile."

These little nuances of body positioning, eye lines, and focal points add endless depth to the simplest of moves and can help your students feel like performers from the very early days.

FANTASY VERSUS FACT: THE HISTORY OF BELLY DANCE

In this internet age, it is not hard to find good hard facts about belly dance and deliver those to our students in an accessible way. Yet we still see myth presented as truth. As teachers we each have a duty to pass our learning history on to our students. Each teacher will have a slightly different style to teach and her own history to bring to the mix. Look critically at your past teachers and the history that they taught. If they came from a culture where belly dance was done in every home, then you can assume their thoughts on that culture are solid. However, if they have never performed in public, then you may need to speak to someone who understands that part of belly dance. Your previous teacher may have learned an imported style of belly dance, and you may want to present a more local accent to your students. Perhaps they are under the spell of a particular dance guru or have a very open interpretation of what is and isn't belly dance. Now is a wonderful time to chat with other dancers and find out about their history, knowledge, views, and interests.

There are many teachers who have focused their life's work on one aspect or topic in belly dance, and they often have wonderfully detailed websites or offer presentations or discussions as well as workshops. I find it helpful to name my sources in class when I quote them. The students may not know the name, but they will respect you for going to prime sources and sharing that information. Shira has a website to which she invites some very wise people to contribute. Consider, also, some of the magazines both online and in print that accept contributions from experts. Always look to the source when searching for facts. Are the writers talking about their own experience or have they researched their topic in depth and from multiple sources? Or perhaps they are repeating a tale that sounds truer each time it is retold.

One of the problems I have with fantasy is that not everyone will share your interests in a fictional setting or origin. Everyone should respect the facts. If you use images such as the stereotypical harem of cheesy movies, you may be alienating students who feel uncomfortable with that style of dancing. By all means tell your students that you feel a strong connection to the moon, but don't tell them belly dance is about worshiping a moon goddess and leave them open to repeating that idea as the truth. Belly dance has such a huge history and such wonderful meanings for all of us. Teachers have the opportunity to open up all those possibilities to each and every student.

The history of belly dance is a book in itself, and there are a few out there that you can compare. Your style of belly dance will influence the history you teach, but don't be afraid to start with yourself and work backward. Talk about how you found belly dance and your journey from that point. Talk about your teacher and her contributions to the world of belly dance as well as her influence on your style. Next, talk about where she learned to dance, her influences and teachers. Very soon you will be talking about the great dancers and those who introduced belly dance to new areas and audiences.

Remember that before the movies we had no real record of how movements looked. Dances have been described in books for centuries, but usually the writer wanted to present the feel of a performance rather than a handbook for repeating those moves. "She swung like a whirlpool in the murky depths of the Nile" does not indicate the writer was watching a hip rotation; rather, it gives a flavor of her dance being dark and otherworldly. We can guess the dancer's movements, but we cannot be sure.

Dancers love to look back toward the Orientalism of the nineteenth century, with its flavor of the Middle East captured by western travelers. In Orientalism we can find the lives of women who danced, from all classes and from many countries, described in books and paintings. Each one of these has a story to tell, but it is simply one person's story – often told by another – and not the story of a whole dance style. These stories are fascinating and worth sharing, but you should not base your version of belly dance history on just one or two historical characters. Look also at the film stars of the early Egyptian cinema, who can share with us not only their stories but also their dance moves. Beyond the famous names there are hundreds of dancers waiting to demonstrate their style and skills in almost-forgotten movie clips.

It is doubtful that we will ever find the name of the very first belly dancer, or that knowing her or him would solve any of the riddles of where our beautiful dance originated. We don't know what motivated people to dance through the ages and across borders, except that we have all been bitten by that same bug. I find the obsession with early belly dance to be a distraction when we can still buy tickets to see pioneers of belly dance styles, buy their biographies, and speak to those who danced with them twenty, forty, or sixty years ago. Keep an eye out for workshops with dancers willing to share their own histories and those of the dancers they have met. Read widely about the dance styles of each country, and remember to present fact, speculation, and myth to your students with honesty.

126

TEACHING CHOREOGRAPHY

There is nothing so exciting as seeing choreography you wrote performed by dancers you have taught. I must admit to a few occasions of proud tears over the years. The trick to teaching your group choreographies is to keep it a step below what you know they are capable of and give them lots and lots of time to learn and practice, without allowing them to become bored. Get the balance just right, and you will have confident, competent dancers who love performing and engaging the crowd.

Writing choreography is like preparing dessert; you can spend four hours baking a cake, icing it, and cutting up strawberries to decorate, or you can pull the lid off a yogurt carton.

Don't believe me? Here is an instant choreography that works with almost every pop song ever written:

Opening section – improvise
Hip drops
Figure eights
Hip lifts
Rotations
Side-to-side bumps
Snake arms
Repeat from hip drops

Try applying the above instant choreography to popular dance songs like, "Simerik" (Kiss, kiss,) "Shik Shak Shok," "Zeina," or "Chicky" just to name a few. You will quickly get the idea. Of course, the trick here is that I haven't listed how many repetitions of each move you are going to do. You are listening for changes in the music and adjusting your dance moves to fit. It also helps that most pop music layers a beat with a melody through almost every part of the song, so almost any move almost always fits. Pop songs tend to open with either a melody or a beat and then the other joins in, so by asking you to improvise the opening I am doubling the chances of there being a beat for the hip drops.

Please don't write your choreographies like this! When you simply list moves that mostly fit with the music, it becomes hard for the dancers to remember and it is more like a shopping list than choreography. Your choreography has to connect with the music and the dancers in a way that is memorable and interesting.

Similarly, when you write choreography for yourself it may look like this:

Right shoulder forward
Left shoulder forward
Chest up
Roll down
Down right, left, right
Cross right foot over
Chin up
Turn

And that's just the first eight beats. Although this kind of choreography connects to the music and brings it to life perfectly, it would be impossible to teach to a beginners class, unless you were happy to limit your performance to thirty seconds and had plenty of practice time.

When the music repeats in your solos you are probably used to showing moves on different parts of your body or changing your angle to the audience or switching the moves around to show personality. Class choreographies for beginner dancers need to lose some of that character and stick with simplified repeats. If the music goes dum dum-dum, hips go down down-down. Every time. Once your group is more experienced you can add back those layers, turning, level changes, stage positions, but initially, keep it simple.

Limiting the number of times you change a move helps to shorten the shopping list part of learning choreography, but it can also make choreography boring. Eight repeats is fine, sixteen is probably OK too, but if you repeat a move for thirty-two counts you need to add something more interesting to keep the audience's attention. It's much better to repeat a short combination four times, or add some simple changes from left and right:

Four hip drops right, four shoulder hits
Four hip drops left, four shoulder hits
Four hip drops right, four shoulder hits
Four hip drops left, four shoulder hits

Students cope better with combinations that connect with the music than those that don't, but don't overfill your choreography with too many complex nuances just because the music you chose is too complex. Find music that has simple phrases, a good repeating chorus, and one or two highlights that can be featured moments in your performance. If you can't call a combination in time to the music, then it is too complex for this level and needs to be simplified.

> Four hip drops right, four shoulder hits
> Four hip drops left, four shoulder hits
> Figure eight right, left, right, left, right, left
> Turn to the right

Simplifying layers can be a great way to take a solo and turn it into a group number – just as adding layers can upgrade group choreography to be suitable as a solo. Focus on what is most important in that part of the choreography, and limit yourself to that part only. When adding layers for a group performance, you need to be sure that everyone is strong in each layer and can execute them easily (if in doubt, leave it out). Here's an example:

> Four hip drops right forward to back (arms framing the working hip)
> Four shoulder hits turning to the right (arms w)
> Four hip drops left forward to back (arms framing the working hip), four shoulder hits turning to the left (arms w)
> Four hip drops right forward to back (hand pointing to audience), four heel bounces with arms swapping sides
> Four hip drops left forward to back (hand pointing to audience), four heel bounces with arms close and open

When working with groups, arm positions can get terribly messy, and students can become stressed about arm placements, which way their hand is turned, and how many counts to take with an arm lift and fall. For group dances, arms are best placed somewhere and left alone. Pick a good strong frame for each move and work on perfecting that position and the arm transitions between.

Great class choreographies have the perfect mix of repeated patterns, limited changes of move, connection with the music, and simplified layers and arms. Make sure you have one or maybe two moments that will surprise the audience or allow your students to show off a difficult move.

CALCULATING YOUR TIMING

With your choreography written, it is now time to calculate how long it will take you to teach. This will depend on the level of your students, your teaching style, and how well you want them to understand the choreography. I have taught a favorite choreography in the last half hour of class that I also used as the base of a ten-week course. The first group mostly followed me and learned it for fun. The second group was planning to perform in a stage show, and we worked hard on each detail until we had a finely tuned performance to present.

Divide your choreography up into phrases, combinations, or chapters and highlight moves that are new to the group. List the key combinations that will need drilling and the layered moves that need breaking down. Finally, add any other part that you think may be tricky or that you know will need work. Now allocate time for each of those sections.

CHOREOGRAPHING YOUR STUDENTS

Some teachers work on different sections for each lesson, starting with the hardest combination, so that the students have the most time to work on that. Others start with the easy parts so that they can feel they have 90 percent of the dance done before focusing on the hardest 10 percent. Still others like to work from the beginning to the end, adding a new move or two each week.

It helps when adding new sections to the choreography if students have already covered it in the previous class or in the warm-up. My students often laugh (or groan) when the next part of their choreography is the combination we already drilled in the warm-up.

When practicing drills or layers to add to your choreography, mix the speeds, so that they start with a good slow beat but gradually take it up until it is faster than they need to do it in the choreography. That way the choreography music will seem slow and steady, and the dancers won't panic.

Each time you add a new phrase, step aside and watch your dancers so they don't become reliant on watching you when they should be performing. Dance it for them to watch, then dance it with them once or twice before asking them to dance it for you. Choreography needs to settle into the dancers' muscle memory, but if all they learn is how to look at you from every angle, they won't be able to dance it without you.

I am not a big fan of dancing with my students in a performance setting. It is not fair to set your students up as your backing dancers, and no matter how hard you try, a teacher rarely blends into a group, which means the audience is focused just on you and not your students.

I know I can add more to a rehearsal by watching and correcting them from the outside than from practicing alongside them. Think hard before you decide to dance with your group. If they need you because they don't know the dance, then they need more practice. If their performance looks flat without you, then they need more work on their energy and projecting their personalities. For first-time dancers it can be more reassuring to have you stand at the back of the room smiling and putting your thumbs up than to have you on stage with them.

Once your students know their dance, make plenty of time for practice without letting them become too bored. Limit your critiques to just a few things in each run-through, and focus on things that will matter for your performance setting. On a big stage, arm positions become more important, whereas in a cozy club the audience can see every tiny tummy move. Change the formations and face different walls to prepare them for the chance that one of them may be ill or they could end up in a different space than the one they prepared for.

Remember that each student will learn differently, so provide notes but also encourage them to draw pictures, make notes, sketch out phrases, or add in counts that suit their learning style. I like to provide them with two versions of the choreography:

- One with all the tiny details; for example, "Hip rotation, starting on right, forward, left, back, with middle finger on outer edges of the eyebrows, palms in, elbows out, shoulders down, eyes forward"

- One with a few quick cue words; for example, "Hip rotation"

The first version is usually long-winded and covers multiple pages; the second is perfect to pin on the wall in their practice space.

If you encourage your students to be creative, they will present you with some wonderful combinations that you can use in their choreography choruses or openings. It's a fun task to set for your students during an extended holiday to work on twenty seconds of music each, which you can then link together for a student-led choreography and a perfect stepping stone to encouraging them to write their own solos.

TEACHING PERFORMANCE SKILLS

Even if you don't have a performance opportunity for your students, a choreography semester is a good time to start teaching them about performance skills. Beginner students will often tell you that they are never, ever, ever going to dance in front of an audience. (You can remind them of that when they do their first solo. It is one of the perks of the job.) The more confidence you can offer them, the more they will enjoy performing, and even if you are not a regular performer yourself, you have a huge knowledge of the nuts and bolts of bringing dance to a variety of stage settings.

Rehearse the dancers' performance from the moment they leave a dressing room until they return. Teach them how to walk to the stage, how wait and warm up before being introduced, and how to walk to their starting points. You may have a number of "belly dancer walks" that you like to teach, but be sure to add arm positions and posture.

Teach your students how to wait on stage for that seemingly endless three seconds it takes for the music to start and at what points you want them to connect with their audience.

Give them lots of opportunities to dance for each other, to practice smiling and making eye contact.

At almost every event I have ever attended, there has been a problem with music in some way. The music has been either delayed or jumped, or the wrong music has played for someone. Prepare your groups for all these problems so they can continue to perform with confidence. Set rules to follow if the wrong music comes on. Either someone off stage will talk to the stage manager, or the dancer closest to the exit will sweetly glide off and talk to the stage manager or whoever is running the music. In the mean time, one of the dancers should move forward to lead the group in some improvisation. If anyone knows the music that is playing, she will walk confidently to the front. If no one knows the music, then the lead dancer or whoever is in the front at the opening leads the group. Group improvisation for any style can look classy with a confident leader, good cues, framing arms, and limited changes. The hope is that this group improvisation needs to last for only a minute; then the dancers can bow and move back to their start positions to wait for their chosen music to start. The crowd will love to see a group cope without stress in a crisis, and the dancers will love that you prepared them for all eventualities.

Costume malfunctions fall into two categories: ones that don't affect the performance and ones that force the dancer to leave the stage. Teach your students to know the difference and to make the right decision under performance stress. If a shoulder strap comes undone, this may not be a problem on a costume that has a halter neck too, or if the number is nearly over and the dancer can finish with one hand on her heart, or if the toupee tape is holding and there are no shoulder shimmies. However, sometimes a shoulder strap failure means that the dancer needs to smile, bow (while holding everything in place), and exit the stage. If veils become tangled, you may prefer your dancers to continue without their veils rather than pick them up from the floor, but if a veil catches fire (I have seen that happen!), then the number is probably over and the dancers should leave the stage, taking care not to set the whole venue on fire.

Talk about how individual dancers can leave the stage while maintaining belly dancer persona and without drawing too much attention from the others in their group.

Finally, teach your students how you'd like them to bow and take their applause. I like to choreograph their exit to a count:

> Pause, 2, 3, 4
> Hand to heart, 2, 3, 4
> Curtsy and stay down, 2, 3, 4
> Rise, 2, 3, 4
> Open arm, smile, turn, walk off

You may want to write some other combination, but teach them to take their time, and drill them until they do your exit combination in sync. If audiences are going to remember only that last ten seconds of a performance, then it's a good idea to make it look classy and coordinated.

TEACHING EVERYTHING ELSE

The world of belly dance is so interesting and fascinating that just teaching moves and dance doesn't seem to be enough. The main aim for the teacher at the beginner level should be to find out the students' interest and feed that without drowning them in too much information. Try to pick one or two topics that fit in well with the lesson plan. For example, you could talk about folk and folkloric dances while teaching the forward and back step, and use the time spent discussing arm positions to introduce the idea of looking good in photographs. Some topics come up naturally; some are led by the students, others are a great base for a full course of classes.

Only you can decide what is important to you as a dancer and teacher. If you teach ATS you may base your history on the rise in popularity of tribal styles in San Francisco, but if you teach Egyptian style the movie stars of the 1940s will be more important to you. If you teach in New York you may want to take your students on a tour of the old clubs, or perhaps your students are keen to perform and you need to teach them those skills early on along with the ethics to help maintain a strong market in live performers. Your particular priorities and knowledge are what set you apart as a teacher.

Teaching also means constantly learning, so take workshops in topics outside your comfort zones, research online, and ask other teachers for their thoughts.

Here are some further topics to consider including in your courses:

- Choreography writing
- Costuming
- Countries of origin: history, geography, culture
- Dancing in shoes
- Dancing to live music
- Drum patterns
- Drumming
- Duets
- Film stars
- Floor patterns
- Floor work
- Improvisation
- Instruments
- Linking and transitions
- Local pioneers
- Makeup
- Music artists
- Music every dancer should know
- Other belly dance styles
- Performance sets
- Performer promotion
- Posing for photography
- Props
- Song lyrics
- The history of belly dance
- Traditional music
- Veil entrances
- Your personal dance history
- Zills

Each of these topics could easily fill ten hours, yet in some way you will need to touch on them all. I like to focus first on belly dance styles from around the world and through the eras, giving me the chance to mention other topics as they fit in with each. I want my students to be able to watch any video on the Internet and see how it fits into the belly dance world. You may see some of these topics as far more important than others, and that is one way you will set yourself apart from other belly dance teachers.

Add to this list, and the list of belly dance styles that you prepared earlier, as you find other topics that your students may want to learn about. Keep the list handy when deciding what topics to teach throughout each year. In theory you could easily teach for ten years without repeating a topic, but in practice you will find that your students love to learn to dance with the veil, or ask to do more gothic belly dance, allowing you to repeat topics more regularly but in even more depth.

As you study each topic in preparation for teaching a course for your more advanced students, think about developing a workshop that you can offer outside of your area or as part of a local dance event.

PRAISE AND CRITICISM

We all want to get the best out of our students – to turn them into amazing performers, help them lose the extra weight, master that complex layer, or perfect their arm placements – but sometimes we have to stop and notice what it is that they want. When we ask students about their goals and objectives, the most common answer seems to be that they want to have fun. I don't mean that we have to make up silly words to love songs or giggle our way through every drill, but some lightheartedness needs to shine in each of your lessons.

People's reactions to praise and criticism vary widely and may not be a reflection of your teaching in any way. Sadly, many people were bullied as children or had parents who found it hard to be supportive. Some people find themselves in relationships where constant criticism is used as a weapon or in a work situation with very little control over the bigger picture. These people are looking for something they can do well, a place where they can learn in a supportive atmosphere and leave having achieved both your and their goals. They may not equate being critiqued with having fun. That is not to say you cannot provide critique, but always keep your criticism in proportion. Their ugly hip drop is not going to cause anyone to starve nor will it speed up global warming. Part of the reason their hip drop is ugly is because you have not explained it in a way that they can understand at this point in the lesson.

Focus the majority of your negative comments on the whole room and balance private criticism by putting it in a sandwich of praise. For my student with ugly hip drops, I would pause by her as I walk the room and say something like "Arms are much nicer this week; well done. Do you see how your head bounces a bit with each drop? That is probably a mix of having your supporting knee overly bent and not being isolated enough. Keep your chest lifted. Good, that looks much better. How does it feel?"

Then once I am back at the front of the class I can use the opportunity to add to the critique without its being too personal: "I noticed a few people had problems with the isolation. Remember our good posture. Sometimes it's hard to maintain, but it will minimize problems like a head bob, and keeping the supporting knee in posture will protect us from injury. If you bounce up and down with this move, the audience doesn't know where to look. Their eyes are naturally drawn toward the head movement and your eyes, and there is a chance they may miss your beautiful hip drops all together. I also saw beautiful arms when we started out, but once they got tired they went all floppy. Don't think I don't notice how everyone's arms perk up when I walk past! I know you can do amazing arms."

Comments to individuals need to be presented in a way that clarifies that you want to help them improve and that you know they can do what you ask of them. A new dancer may well not be able to give you great posture, an isolated hip drop, pretty arms, interesting fingers, and a relaxed smile and keep time with the music. As a teacher you will need to decide which of these are more important for her to focus on first. If you tell her all the things wrong with her hip drops, she is unlikely to come back next week. Physical safety should always be a priority. Thinking about the same dancer, I am going to remind her about her posture first. If her posture is good, then I want the move we are working on to improve. If the move and posture are good, then it is time to look at her smile, her arms, and then finer details.

However, if you never give any criticism you may find yourself with some blissfully ignorant dancers who believe that everything they do is perfect. After all, if it wasn't, you would have told them, right? Unfortunately, the most deluded dancers tend to be those whose dancing has so many faults that their teacher has struggled to know where to start or has given up correcting. Improving your students' dancing starts with a little step each lesson as we guide them to be the dancers they want to be. If you feel that they don't listen to you, simplify the message. Once you have explained a dozen or more times about how you would like them to hold their arms, you can simply say "Arms" as you travel the room, then move on. This reinforces the message that their dancing is not perfect and what the specific problem is; it also turns the process over to them; if they really can't remember what it is about their arms that you want them to improve, they must approach you and ask for a more detailed critique.

Praise the whole group as the lesson ends or at the end of a task. A simple "Well done everyone, you all worked hard" can go a long way toward motivating your students.

It is important to not have favorites. Try to make sure every dancer gets her share of praise and encouragement. Praise to part of the group can seem like a criticism to the others unless you focus on being even-handed. To say "The front row had exceptional tummy flutters today" may come across as highlighting a problem with the flutters among the back row students, who feel unappreciated. It may be that they need to work on their tummy flutters too, but if so, then say that and sandwich it with some other praise: "The front row had exceptional tummy flutters today. Back row needs to practice those for homework, please. But good job, everyone – the turns are looking fabulous."

ONE-ON-ONE CRITIQUE

Students will sometimes ask for critique or a private lesson aimed at improving their dance. Critique is a great way to grow as a dancer, but both the student and the teacher need to set some ground rules before a critique session. This can be done fairly simply with a questionnaire or with a quick email to the student before a critique session to make sure you both want to cover the same topics and agree on the level of improvement the student is looking for. A beginner who wants a critique on how to become a pro dancer is going to want lots of generalizations and to leave with a plan of activities to work on over the next year or two. A performer who wants help on a choreography she hopes to dance in a competition next week is looking for you as a teacher to be very picky and pull her up on the fine details.

Again, when working on a critique it is best to think about how you can phrase each problem in a way that won't crush the dancer and will inspire her to improve. Without a class full of students to aim your generalizations at, turn the conversation to what many other dancers do: "I have noticed lots of dancers tend to walk, twirl, walk when they enter the stage with a veil, so maybe you could think of something more interesting that will catch the judges' eye right from the start."

Use the dancer's strengths to balance her weaknesses: "You look so beautiful when you stand center stage and really own that space; maybe you could cut back on the travelling and make more of a feature of that skill."

Balance your feedback, being mindful of how much time the dancer has to make those improvements: "Try shifting some of those drumbeats into your shoulders for variety, and maybe over the next few months we can work on other places you can mark a beat so you feel more confident with chest lifts or tummy work. For now, I think a weight shift would change how the audience sees those drops happen and be a great way to make it really interesting."

Always aim to finish your private lesson and critique on a high note. You can list all the things that you have covered in your session and also the things that you love about the dancer. If she is preparing for a performance or competition, make sure she knows that you are confident in her abilities and that she already has everything she needs to be amazing. Think of praising her smile, confidence, or stage presence in addition to the work she has done.

I would never offer a critique that wasn't asked for and certainly not close to a performance date. Nothing will crush a potential performer more than believing that you think their work can be fixed only by spending an hour or two with you.

OPEN-ENDED QUESTIONS

To help develop creative, expressive, and mindful dancers, we must give them permission to think for themselves and move away from simply echoing our styling back at us. I find one of the best ways to introduce this transition is with open-ended questions.

The most obvious open-ended question for dancers is "How does that feel?"

With an open-ended question there is no right answer. The verbalizing is not important and tells us very little, but the process of thinking – in this example, "How does it feel?" – is the key factor.

The students may reply "Stiff," or "Gooey" or "Liquid," which gives you a clue to what they are thinking, but ideally their thoughts go much deeper than that. They might be thinking that they feel like a river flowing around rocks, or they may be reminded of playing hula hoop as a child. Maybe they are thinking of the way that jam bubbles and boils in the pot, or the tingle of the shower first thing in the morning. Very few students will feel brave enough to paint a beautiful, poetic picture of all the ways that belly dance plays with the senses, but by asking them we give their imagination permission to expand.

Practical Tip:

Do a few chest circles and figure eights in place. How does it feel? Describe the feelings as a movement. Explain to me how it feels with a visual answer. How does it make you feel emotionally? Is it sensual? What fabric would a chest circle be? Is it silk, or wool, velvet, or felt? How does a chest circle smell or taste? Is it like chocolate or coffee, carrots or cheese? How foolish do you feel trying to find answers to these questions?

Understanding how foolish it feels to be asked and to not have an answer to a question like "Is a chest circle like cheese?" reminds us how our students feel when we ask them about their dancing. They may want to answer you straight – "It feels like my chest is going around in circles" – and that is not a wrong answer. They may want to say, "It feels like a warm beach at sunset. My breathing is the waves gently breaking over driftwood and pebbles. My shoulders are warm, but relaxed as if they are enjoying the cooling sun. My heart aches to watch the sun go down, marking the end of a perfect day, but the circles remind me that tomorrow, and tomorrow and tomorrow there will be a sunset for me to enjoy."

It is up to you to work on making the classroom space safe enough for them to verbalize all those feelings and to share them with their classmates.

The first way you can help your students to express their feelings and to think deeply about each move is to do it yourself, but don't force your feelings on them. A quick "I always feel really young and youthful doing this move" is fine.

Second, accept their thoughts, no matter how strange they may sound. We all express ourselves differently, and their feedback may help others find the depths that you cannot reach.

Third, encourage deeper thinking about their movement. A journey from A to B is just as much about the turns and bumps in the road as it is about the departure and arrival. Ask students to take notice of all the parts of their movement and also how isolated body parts play their role. Offer them contrasts to consider, like a big figure eight next to a small one, a fast followed by a slow, an isolated against a more relaxed. Ask them to contrast how they feel.

Finally, offer up a variety of open-ended questions. Simply rephrasing your question may help them understand what it is that you want them to do and stimulate different types of answers.

Here are some questions to ask at the end of drills and combinations and after learning new moves:

- How are you feeling after that?
- Where is your weight centering?
- Where is the smoothest part of that move?
- How would a tempo change affect that?
- Where do you ache?
- Where is that movement building from?
- Where did your weight shift?
- Was the beat or melody distracting?
- How did the lyrics change your dancing?
- Did you feel moody, emotional, powerful, childish, crushed?
- Did that music give you energy?
- When you are isolating, which body parts want to join in? What happens when you let them? How does that change the move?
- Are you building warmth in any part of your body? Is it like a glow or a passionate heat?
- How can you keep the posture and still relax and enjoy dancing?
- How did your dancing improve in the last three minutes?
- What move would make that combination feel more complete?
- How would you change that to be more suitable for a large theater stage or a small intimate restaurant?
- If you could change one arm position, what would it be?
- How could you turn with that combination?
- If you were dancing a duet, how would you change it to play up each dancer's skills?
- Does that combination suit you?

By asking lots of questions, you not only encourage your dancers to think about their moves but also give them permission to be creative. After a while they will admit to thinking, while drilling a move, "What is my teacher going to ask? How do I feel? Where is my weight? Where is the flow? How would I change it?"

You will also find lots of inspiration for your Ta-dah! moments at the end of the lessons. If the dancers are full of ideas after a combination, give them the time and space to change it to better suit themselves, or divide them into groups to change the arm positions or to travel. You can bring flash cards with an extra move to add, a performance setting to try, or an emotion to layer over the top.

If you don't have time this week, consider adding it to your plan for next week. A quick revisiting of the combination at the beginning of the lesson helps call it back from memory and links the two lessons together.

TEACHING SMALL GROUPS

When you're first starting out as a belly dance teacher, you may have lessons when no one shows up, or you have to teach to a class of one or two. If this happens, don't be too disappointed; take advantage of the opportunity to work with those dancers in more detail, by asking them if they have skills they want to master and deviating slightly from the lesson plan. One day, when your room is packed at every lesson, you will remember how it was when no one came to your first few classes.

With a smaller group you can teach from one centered spot and remain there for most of the lesson. This helps the students to own their own space and to keep the same view of you for the whole lesson. Don't be surprised if students like their spot so much that they arrive early to claim it each week for years. You can shuffle them around a little to do partner work or for their choreographies, but they will probably drift back to their preferred place. It may be that they position themselves so that their stronger ear is toward the music or so that you are the right distance away from the mirror for their vision.

You can move a small class into a circle for some work, but some people feel exposed by a circle formation because everyone can see everyone else, and in a small group it's easy to feel insecure. Give them a clear floor pattern for travelling moves, and take advantage of the space to dance across the floor in diagonals as well as straight toward the mirror.

If your room is oversized for your group, consider allocating only part of it for your class. Move everyone onto the stage, or center yourself in front of a large window, subtly reducing the working floor space into a more manageable area.

Small classes seem to lack energy, and it is hard to make them fun. Judge your students' needs just as you would a larger class, and change the tone of your music to suit. Don't let your nerves show by trying too hard to be humorous or to pack your lesson with too many activities. Some of my best lessons as a student were in the small classes. The paying customers deserve the best of you in each and every lesson, even if it is hard to forget that your hall hire is costing you twice your income in that hour. As you'll see in the next section, someday you may be looking back with wistful fondness at the space and tranquility of your small classes!

TEACHING LARGE GROUPS

We have all been there, whether as students or teachers: that moment when you arrive at a workshop to see a sea of students already filling every available space. It is a curse as a student, but I hope it's a blessing for you as a teacher, as you get to share your wisdom with many people all at the same time.

When space is at a premium it is only fair to move everyone around periodically to allow for each student to spend some time with a good view. Sometimes it can be easier to move you than it is to move a large number of people.

Perhaps the most commonly used way to shuffle students around is the "front to back," where you send the front two rows back and everyone else takes a couple of steps forward. Although this gives everyone the chance to be near the front at some point, it does have its disadvantages. Often the dancers who start off at the back may have done so by choice, so moving them forward where others can see them making mistakes can make them nervous and more prone to blunders. There will always be a few who think your rearrangements don't include them and who continue to stay at the front as others move forward, creating a roadblock. It also causes constant reshuffling as the second row dancers put themselves in the gaps between the first, and then the third row dancers all have to shift to see, then the fourth, and the fifth – and by the time the back row dancers have organized themselves, it is time to move the front row back again. I find as a teacher I am looking out at a mass of fidgeting dancers, and the vibe can get angry as the lady with the huge hair wrap sways from side to side and the rest of the room sways in the opposite direction to keep you, the teacher, in view.

145

It can be easier to move yourself from the center of the front wall to the side wall, back wall, and other side so that the students just turn 90 degrees each time. That doesn't help if you like to call "arm to the clock" rather than "arm to the right diagonal, slightly in front," but you can make that adjustment. Sometimes students feel more familiar with their right and left if you stay facing the same way all the time, but they will soon get used to this method of viewing the teacher. To help organize the room and to cover as I scurry from one wall to the next, I ask them all to take a few steps forward (filling the space I was using), turn 90 degrees to face the new wall, then take a few steps back (to give me space to dance).

If you have a raised platform or stage in your space, then being higher makes you easier to see. Unfortunately, it also makes you less accessible and puts a barrier between you and your students. I do find that students who learn this way have wonderful neck lines from always looking up as they dance! Make sure you have some way to get up and down easily, so that you can make adjustments privately and you don't end up shouting, "You, in the green! Your arms!"

Circles can be a surprisingly good way to teach a large group, if the space allows. It's the best way to have a long front row, and if you set up an inner and outer circle everyone has a good view of you. This doesn't work so well if you are teaching a combination with directions, but it is excellent for stationary work and travelling drills. Do not overfill your circles or your students will be pushed to the outer edges of the room and end up walking into shoes or bags or stacks of chairs that litter the outer edges of your room. If you plan on making two or three circles, call people out by what they are wearing rather than trying to impose some complex system such as "every third person take two steps in." Remember, your view of the room is different from theirs. You can usually split out two-thirds of your students for an outer circle by asking everyone "not wearing black" to step in three steps. You can also do a rough count of how many are wearing coin belts or have their hair up and use that as a way to split them up.

When doing travelling steps, go the opposite way from the students so that you can see them all and they get to see you at different angles. It's nice, once you've gotten them into a circle formation, to see how much of the lesson you can teach without having to move them. For example, if you wanted to teach a combination with travelling and stationary components, you could adapt it slightly so that the two circles travel in opposite directions (one going clockwise, the other counterclockwise) for a count of eight and then turn to face the other circle before dancing the stationary moves, making eye contact with a new partner each time.

TEACHING EXTREMELY LARGE GROUPS

Sometimes the number of people who attend a class or workshop just doesn't work in the area you have. Perhaps you misjudged the size of the room or dozens of people unexpectedly turned up. If so, nice job on the publicity! Now make sure you apologize and promise to make changes so that it doesn't happen again.

For a class, you can try to arrange two classes the following week. If it's a workshop, then sell tickets in advance, decide on a final number, and stick to it for next time. Sometimes, despite your best efforts to avoid it, you have to teach a huge group. First, look for other options. Can you swap class room with someone else in the building or move your group to an open space outside? Next, adjust your lesson plan to suit the situation. Travelling in complex patterns will be annoying, so show once how you would like it done and then ask the group to mark it in place. Get a microphone and talk in detail, giving a more in-depth lesson, but with less dancing. Your dancers may be happy to divide their time between dancing and watching, so split the group in half and send them to two sides of the room. Stand in front of the first group, facing the second, but ask that only the first group dance with you. After a minute or two, turn around and ask the first group to walk back to their wall and allow the second group to fill in the space so they can take their turn to dance. Stay with the second group to add a new move or combination and then swap them again. That way everyone gets to dance and to watch.

Of course, if you know you are going to get huge numbers, then you can see up a video screen and project your teaching. The screen creates even more distance between the students and their teacher, you may wonder how much more teaching each dancer is getting than they might get from buying your DVD. Make sure to keep it personal to make each student feel like she had her fair share of your time.

You may be lucky enough to have a student or partner who is willing to be your body for the back of the class or to help students see the dance from different angles. This is really important if your choreography faces different walls, but you may still find your students watching you over their shoulder rather than facing your helper. Be sure your helper is willing to help. It can be really boring and annoying to be asked to assist with choreography you already know when you have paid to be a participant and learn some new content. Students who help the teacher more than they learn should be paid or at least attend the class or workshop for free.

ADAPTING FOR MIXED-LEVEL CLASSES

No matter how small a class you teach, you will always have to make adaptations to your lesson plan for students of different levels. Even in a week one beginners class, you could have a professional salsa dancer standing next to someone who was told she couldn't dance at age six and has not so much as tapped her toes since. You might find yourself challenged to teach graceful arms to a total beginner and a dancer with ten years of belly dance performance behind her. If possible, it's a lot easier to offer more than one class and aim those classes at different levels of student. However, many teachers plan a mixed-ability class to save on time or room hall costs, deliberately choosing to have beginners learn next to advanced students.

Teaching mixed-level classes comes with its own set of challenges, which can be great fun or may crush the passion you have for teaching belly dance. In some cases you can simply set up a move or exercise, explain it to suit each learning style, and then walk the room giving advice to each of your students to suit their own ability. Other times you will have to divide the group and set up adaptations.

Adaptations are simply different ways to do the same move or concept in a way more suited to the dancers' skill levels. The easiest way to do this is with layers. For example, if you were teaching figure eights to your mixed-ability class, you could break down the move and ask the beginners to repeat the basic move. You could ask those who are happy with figure eights to isolate them, add arms, or add a backward shoulder roll, a forward shoulder roll, a shimmy, or a chest circle. Adding arms or a shimmy is fairly easy and would be fine for someone with a few months' experience. Adding the chest circle is really hard and would be suitable only for students with great posture and confidence in both moves. This kind of layering up is a wonderful way to challenge all of your students but can be a little boring for them. Try not to use it more than once in each lesson.

More interesting for the dancers is any adaptation that involves their imagination or their own creativity with existing skills; perhaps asking them to follow the melody in a complex piece of music or to switch among figure eights, reverse figure eights, mayas, and reverse mayas as the music leads them.

Finally, splitting up the group gives you smaller groups or pairs who can work together with adaptations. You can ask the groups to be creative and come up with their own combination starting with figure eights, or to set up a duet in which one leads with figure eights on the hips while the other complements her with flowing arms. If you pair up more advanced dancers with beginners, you can challenge the advanced dancers to mirror everything the beginners do with their hips but with chest moves. Keep mixing it up and thinking of new, fun ways to keep all your dancers learning.

Let your dancers find their own levels. Sometimes an experienced dancer will lack confidence in a core move and want to drill it with the beginners rather than add layers or add in the adaptations. Allow them to make their own choices, as long as they know there are more challenges if they want some.

Try to think of a few adaptations as you write your lesson plan, even if it's just a theoretical exercise to begin with. There will be occasions when you will be grateful to have some ideas tucked away and can make a simple lesson more fun for a surprise attendee.

CONTINUOUS CLASSES

Continuous classes are those not set to a term or semester, with no start and no finish, where new students can join at any point. This approach has the advantage of getting new customers for your business into the habit of attending class right from the moment they first show an interest, rather than waiting for a new course to start. The disadvantages include huge potential problems with the dancers and class as a whole never moving forward. If you take the time in each lesson to cover posture and a few basic moves for the new students, you can never get onto more advanced moves or interesting combinations for the more advanced dancers. Continuous classes can easily stagnate and students get bored with belly dance. Making constant adaptations can really help, but without knowing ahead of time who will attend these classes, they become hard to preplan.

I prepare with a revolving class plan for my continuous classes which works very well for both me and the students. Start by planning the continuous classes with a two or three-month plan that's the equivalent of a term or semester plan. For each lesson plan an introduction to a basic move (and list a second move that can be added if time allows), an interesting way to recap last week's new move, a shimmy exercise, and then the Ta-dah! moment when all the ingredients from the class can be put together.

Here is a simple outline of a continuous course two-month plan. You will notice that the classes have names of colors rather than numbers and that the week after Blue you can teach Green again:

Green:
Warm-up
Revisit last week – chest work
This week – hip rotations (optional shoulder rolls)
Layer up – chest 3D, counterclockwise and clockwise (camel, rib rotation, circles)
Ta-dah! – taqsim "Hip rotation, hip rotation, chest rotation, chest rotation" with speed variations
Shimmies – over chest slides
Cooldown

Red:
Warm-up
Revisit previous week – hip rotation
This week – forward and back step (optional 3/4 walking)
Layer up – travelling, pivoting, and/or corkscrewing rotations
Shimmy – over a hip rotation
Ta-dah! – piece of pop that does some four-count beat and then some fast melody (free dance or repeat a combo)
Cooldown

Violet:
Warm-up
Revisit last week – forward and back
This week – backward horizontal figure 8 (optional 3/4 shimmies)
Layer up – travelling forward and back, adding frame and flow arms
Shimmy – over hips forward and back
Ta-dah! – mixing speed of figure eights with regular beat of forward and back; invent your own arm frame for body type
Cooldown

Yellow:

Warm-up

Revisit last week – figure eight

This week – hip drop (optional belly dancer walks)

Layer up – reverse figure eight (forward horizontal) – emotional difference between the two

Shimmy – detailed explaination and breakdown

Ta-dah! – mirroring each other (your forward is my back), mirror arms or duets

Cooldown

White:

Warm-up

Revisit last week – hip drop

This week – maya (optional vine steps)

Layering up – hip drops patterns, half moon, McDonald, back/forward

Shimmy – layered on different parts of the body

Ta-dah! – swing (double drop travelling backward)

Cooldown

Purple;
Warm-up
Revisit last week – maya
This week – hip lift (optional floor patterns)
Layering up – vertical figure eight (inward maya), hankie hands, undulating with maya and vertical, staccato maya.
Shimmy - layered over weight shift
Ta-dah! – change game (stand in circle, everyone does maya or vertical and you have to change direction without anyone noticing)
Cooldown

Orange:
Warm-up
Revisit last week – hip lift
This week – camel (optional tribal styling)
Layering up – tribal hip lift, travelling, pivoting
Shimmy – with snake arms
Ta-dah! – basic tribal improvisation (introduce idea of group improvisation, camel, hip lift, maya, snake arms) or "follow me" improvisation
Cooldown

Lime:
Warm-up
Revisit last week – camel
This week – side to side (optional arm frames)
Layering up – double camels (two on each side), going up on toes, speed changes
Shimmy – layered onto a walk
Ta-dah! – drill outward and inward double camels with outward and inward arms
Cooldown

Blue:
Warm-up
Revisit last week – side to side
This week – chest slides and good chest posture, (optional umi/omi/internal circle)
Layering up – double side to sides, with snake arms (hips to beat, arms/chest to soft), sharp vs gentle side to side
Shimmy – modulate your speed
Ta da! – cha-cha (123 step) travelling (add side to side if possible)
Cooldown

This can now become a rotating set of topics that you can repeat forever with a little adaptation to keep things fresh. New students still get to do hip rotations within the first ten weeks of taking your class, but long-term students only have to drill the basic moves for ten minutes of the class and then everyone gets to move on to something interesting and challenging. Some weeks you will cover all the layering ideas, next time you might want to look at just one in more depth.

Explain to your students that each lesson starts off with basic drills, then moves on to something harder and finishes with a challenge. Beginners will focus more on the opening section of the class; more advanced dancers will look forward to each challenge. You can easily adapt the class to the mix of students that attend by extending the recap and work on the new move if the class is mostly people who have not done them before, or moving on to the layers and Ta-dah! sooner if no one needs the recap.

I have not included any improvisation or free dance in this plan, but I would use that to finish a class if I had time left over, or divide the class by ability, adding shimmy layers or asking for creativity from my more advanced students.

It is nearly impossible to teach choreography as part of an ongoing class, by its very nature. I would suggest you plan occasional mini workshops for your continuous students where those who have repeated the pattern once or twice can focus on choreography or a topic in more detail.

COVERING CLASS

Inevitably there will be occasions when you cannot make your class and need to find a cover teacher. Prepare for this ahead of time, and your classes can continue without a hitch. Teachers who often cancel or send a substitute teacher without warning can alienate their students, so if you do have time to inform the class in advance, do so.

In case you have to cancel at the last minute, make sure you have contact details for your venue and all of your students. I once had a minor car accident on the way to class. All I could do was telephone the venue and ask them to apologize to the students as they arrived. The venue couldn't open up without the renter (me) on site, so the students couldn't practice that night; instead, they headed off to a nearby café for a social evening, which I believe they enjoyed with a glass of wine.

It is worth checking with your venue when you book whether they will allow an unsupervised practice in the room without you, but don't assume that your students will want to do this.

Avoid putting a senior student in charge of your class too often, or you may find yourself co-teaching and pulling the class apart with your different priorities. Let students take turns leading subgroups under your supervision and enjoy fueling your classes with their ideas while you still maintain your control, leadership, and management.

Local teachers are often happy to help out a fellow teacher by subbing, and if you can approach them with the frame of a lesson plan, it saves them time and effort. Try to tell them where the students are in their learning and what you would like them to learn, but also leave the substitute enough room to teach in her own style. If you teach Turkish style belly dance, the students may love a week of dark gothic dance or ATS, but don't expect those teachers to teach with a Turkish flavor. If your dancers are in the middle of choreography, it may be better to miss a week of practice or simply give the students the chance to dance it through a couple of times without adding anything new. I have been the substitute teacher a couple of times with a group that was midway through a choreography, and I was happy to just keep playing the same section of music while they drilled, because that is what their regular teacher had asked me to do. I made minor corrections and gave them some ideas to help them remember their choreography, but it was not the most exciting lesson I have ever taught.

Equally, it is kind of you to be available to substitute for other local teachers from time to time. Ask for as much information ahead of time as you can get while still being sympathetic to the original teacher's reason for missing her class. If she has had a death in the family, simply say "Yes" and sort the rest out yourself.

It is a good idea to have a couple of quick lesson plans printed up and music already loaded on your phone and iPod so that you are ready to teach at a moment's notice. Here are some tips:

Pick a fun, predictable piece – Choose music that will work with a mix of moves and use that music as your Ta-dah! at the end of your lesson. Load three pieces of music with regular beats and slow melodies to which you can teach almost anything, then use those three moves in an improvisation or combination to your Ta-dah! music. This gives you the chance to stick to the lesson plan that the regular teacher has asked you to teach but to add your own accent.

Moving Accross the Floor – Pick your favorite music for across the floor and use that as a way to find out each dancer's favorite dance step. If someone picks something the others don't know, break it down before adding it to the combination. If they all know each of the moves, then add in your styling, arms, or attitude. Once they tire of travelling across the floor, split them into groups to use the combination to travel in floor patterns as pairs or trios.

Posture and Walking – Everyone needs to work harder on posture and walks. Practice some posture drills, strengthening exercises, and walking with grace. This works well with a group of dancers who are in the middle of choreography as good practice for entering or exiting the stage.

Teach a mini workshop – Take your hot topic and present the material in a mini workshop intensive format.

Focus on Structured Improv – Select a short piece of music or one with regular repeats. Teach a short choreography to the chorus or opening, then split the group into subgroups and ask them to choreograph the rest of the music. It helps if you can bring a printout with the timings already marked. Teaching them the chorus will help you divide up the class by ability. End by asking each group to perform to the others.

Here is a checklist for information you may need from the regular class teacher:

- Directions to the venue, parking instructions, public transport
- Keys, key codes, directions within the building
- Contact details for staff on site
- Onsite music player, quirks of the room, fire exits, heating, air conditioning
- Who to take money from, how much, and how you will split it between you and the regular teacher
- The class level and their midterm goals
- What the class did last week
- What the class must cover this week
- What the class enjoys
- Start and finish times
- Locking-up instructions

Practical Tip:

Take a moment and prepare an email or a sheet of paper that answers these questions about your regular classes as if you were asking someone to cover your class. Each year, review and make changes so that if you do ever need a substitute for one of your classes you already have handy all the information she could need.

STUDENTS AS FRIENDS

Like many of you, I find that most of my friends have come to me through my love of belly dance. I hope that your classes will soon fill up with wonderful, interesting, funny people you want to get to know better and spend time with.

As all teachers know, there is a tiny, invisible wall between those who teach and those who learn. These people pay you to be friendly as well as to impart your wisdom, and while that friendship is mostly real, it is never quite balanced. No matter how much you like your students, they look to you to make the hard calls: to tell a dancer that her skirt is too see-through, or to ask another dancer to try and arrive on time to class.

It's a tough lesson to learn, but don't fall in love with your students too hard. It can be heartbreaking when your best belly dance buddy suddenly quits and removes you from her social network site for no real reason. But it does happen, and it's not always personal. As your students' belly dance teacher, you are one and the same with their love of belly dance. When they fall for salsa or kick boxing or a new lover, something has to give. Picture your group performing at the big local event next year, but don't build your whole choreography around your student who can unicycle. She may not be there. Enjoy today with the students you have, and look forward to tomorrow with whoever chooses your class in the future.

END OF TERM/SEMESTER

Toward the end of your semester you will need to sell your students on the idea of returning and rebooking. Many of us hate to be a salesperson, but returning students are a large part of our market, and I have found them to be my main source of new students. It is best to be honest; tell them that this is your finest hard sell and hand them extra copies of your business cards to pass on to friends.

Return to your original aims for the course and discuss how far you have come, what moves the attendees have covered, and praise the students for all their hard work. A quick list of the moves and concepts gives your students the chance to ask questions or to recover something they missed or didn't understand. If you taught choreography, you can put on a mini show for each other; if you have been working on drum solos or a style of belly dance, you can divide them up into groups to create something challenging. Finish with a giant Ta-dah! moment.

There will always be a few students you never see again. Maybe they are moving halfway around the world, or want to give knitting or Spanish a try next semester. Maybe they have a huge report due in at work; maybe they feel that belly dance is not for them. Whatever the reason, I think it is fair to finish the term with a short talk about their continued journey as a belly dancer, even if that journey is not with me. I talk about how to find other teachers and what level of class I suggest they try. I also explain how they can best describe their belly dance experience to a new teacher, using common terms such as layering, combinations, linking, and improvisation. If they see performance in their future, I tell them their best route, be that through classes with me or with someone else. Performance is a big part of being a belly dancer, and we should not be surprised when dancers are keen to take restaurant jobs or other performance opportunities. A great teacher neither holds her students back nor pushes them forward and can always find a tactful way to tell the enthusiasts if they are not yet ready.

Make sure your students know when and where your next group of classes will be running, and ask them to tell their friends. Offer them an incentive, like a free class, if they bring a friend or promote you via their social networks.

Hand out reenrollment forms at the end of the lesson or offer to take their booking if possible. They are excited about belly dancing in that moment, and it saves them remembering to do it at another time. If the booking doesn't open for a few weeks, tell them that you will be emailing them the details soon, and make sure you have current contact details for them.

Finally, you may want to offer them a verbal or written review of their dancing. Again, follow the sandwich approach to critique, telling them about their most improved skill, the thing they need to work on, and the skill that makes them stand out from the crowd.

FUN AND GAMES

In this section I offer a list of games to play at the end of lessons or at the end of a term. Different people have different ideas of fun: for some, a seven-minute shimmy drill is a great laugh, while other people are looking for party games. Any exercise that makes the dancers laugh is perfect. I have included some drills that are lighthearted and experiments that are easy and don't necessarily fulfill a clear aim. Have fun inventing your own, take these as a starting point, and have a laugh finding out what works for your students.

Seesaw — Split the class into pairs, each facing each other. One dancer does simple hip drops on the right while the other does hip lifts on her left. Repeat until the partners have completed a perfect set of eight on each side (one lifting, the other dropping). Now swap, so the dropper is now lifting and the lifter is now doing hip drops. Repeat the count of eight before swapping sides, then fours, twos, and finally singles. Add arms. People tend to find it instinctive to mirror (both doing drops at the same time), so this exercise is harder than it sounds.

Veil Weightlifting — Start with all the students in a circle. With a bag full of veils, find your own place in the circle. Pull out one veil and ask a dancer next to you to twirl it once around her body and pass it on as seamlessly as she can. As you watch the veil travel around the circle, pick out another veil and hold it in your arms. When the first veil is passed to you, hold it with the second, twirl them (double veils style), and pass both on to the next person. Repeat this process, adding an extra veil each time they come back to you. If you have a large circle, you don't have to wait for the first veil to do a full trip around, just send off another veil whenever you feel like it. After a minute or two, switch directions so everyone twirls equally right to left and left to right.

Murder in the Dark — Dancers stand in small groups of four or five and are allowed to do only figure eights and reverse figure eights. They can add rise and fall, fancy arms, or turns, but they must keep their hips moving. The aim is to change the direction of the figure eights without anyone else seeing. Dancers watch each other's hips, and when they see a change of direction they point, or shout "Murder in the dark!" and the "victim" has to stand still with her hands on her hips until she sees someone else change direction. If someone catches all her teammates, she wins. (However, no one ever seems too concerned about winning or keeping score with this one.)

Capture the Flag — Pair off the dancers into pairs of a similar height and get them to connect together by putting their arms around each other's waists. Dancers on the right of each pair are flags, so give them each a coin belt or a small scarf. Dancers on the left are thieves. The aim of the game is for each pair to travel using only one move (forward and back step, traveling shimmies, hip lifts) so that their thief can steal another group's flag, while keeping their own flag safe. When they steal a flag, the losing team joins the winning team (arm around a waist), and the thief moves on to try to take another flag. In the end everyone will be part of one long line. On the right you can see dancers enjoying this game.

Belly Dance Races — Mark out a square in your dance space, or just ask all the dancers to imagine that the room is one lap and space themselves out around the lap. Using only your chosen travelling move, they have to complete a lap but constantly face the front of the room. This means they will travel forward, sideways, backward, and sideways again. It is a simple race to complete a lap. Dancers overtaking should take a step inward and keep going. To keep everyone safe, make sure the dancers travelling backward have a good view of the mirror or stand along that side yourself.

Grandmother's Shopping List — Stand the dancers in a circle and ask them to think of a move they love (it may be useful to ask them to think of several, or to place your least experienced students on your left so that they have their turn early in the game). Start the game with a good basic move that is easy to link to other moves. Once everyone is in sync and appears comfortable, ask the person on your left to add a new move. Start over and do your move four times, and then the second move. Now ask the next dancer to add a move. Start over and do your move four times, the second move four times and then add on the third. The aim is to remember the moves only by looking at the dancer who picked it. By doing only four repeats, you keep the game fast and fresh. Once everyone has added a move, narrow the repeats to two, then eliminate again, so that you do a single repeat of each move.

Musical Statues — Dancers pick two poses that suit their body type and dance persona. Split the group into pairs and have them spend some time working on their best photo poses together. Once they have two perfect poses, play some slow music and give them time to flow from one pose to the other while taking a step forward: Pose one, move and step, pose two, move and step . . .

As they repeat this, turn the music off at random points so that they have to freeze mid-step. The dancers learn about linking between poses and making sure that they look beautiful even as they move or change. In belly dance every moment has to be photo worthy.

Twisted Twister — Buy an old set of the Twister game and change the body parts from right hand, left hand, right foot, left foot, to body parts that we use in belly dance. I suggest hips, chest, arms, and feet. Then allocate a shape or move to each color: maybe red is circles, blue is eights, yellow is shimmies, and green is a straight line. Each dancer takes it in turn to spin the pointer and dance the move with that part of her body. So she spins red hips and does a hip rotation, or she spins yellow arms and does an arm shimmy. Once everyone understands the game, you can ask them all to layer the last move with the new one, so they are doing an arm shimmy with their hip rotation. They can layer the last three moves or four . . .

The Welcome Game — Find an upbeat piece of music with a repetitive beat and something special on the fourth or eighth count. Something like dum, dum, dum, BOOM! would be ideal. Start the group moving around the room with three steps and a hip lift (step, step, step, lift). If you are doing this with beginners, end each set of counts with a clap (step, step, step, clap). Once the dancers are happy with the beat, change the fourth action. Try a chest lift (step, step, step, chest), or pointing at their nose (step, step, step, nose). On its own this can be lots of fun; you can pull flash cards to give them their next move or come up with lots of silly ideas. If you want to encourage your students to interact with each other, you can change up the fourth move to include high fives, tapping each other on the shoulder, making eye contact, or offering a gift hand (palm open toward the other dancer). This now moves the dancers into closer proximity, more like how they would dance as a troupe, and makes them aware of others around them. As a final twist you can play a version of "rock, paper, scissors" in which each dancer has the first three counts to pick out a partner, and on the fourth count they both do a move from a shortened list (I like gift hand, high five, and clap); if they both do the same move, they lose a life. If they lose three lives they are out. You will be amazed to see how the dancers find it impossible not to mirror each other's moves, and most of them are out within the first five repeats.

KEEPING STUDENTS SAFE

When you are the class teacher, many aspects of the students' safety suddenly become your responsibility. Initially it's a good idea to make sure the room you are using is safe and fit for the purpose. Check that the floor is clean and free from hazards like clothing, bags, or power cables. Check for any wet patches; it could be that the air conditioning is leaking or the previous class got really sweaty. Locate the fire exits and check that they are not locked. If you are on the ground floor, find out how far the windows open, should you need to exit that way. In large buildings reaching the exit may mean crossing a rooftop or climbing down a ladder, so check that all your students would be able to do that, or find alternate routes. Many of us dance barefoot and leave our handbags in lockers, so in an emergency the class teacher may have to encourage students to leave more quickly than they wish and to leave belongings behind. Explore the nearby rooms in case your fire exit is unsafe when you need to use it. Keep some record of all your students with you at all time and take a roll call at the beginning of each lesson in case emergency staff need contact details or to know who was in the building with you.

It's unfortunate but true that you must consider the possibility of random attacks such as shootings or bomb threats; your students would look to you to shepherd them to safety, remain with them, and act as a contact for first responders, so keep a charged-up phone with you and think about your options. Check with your venue and ask to be told before any fire drill, so that you can act promptly should the alarms go off during your class.

It is wise to take a short course in first aid before starting to teach class, but it is equally important to know the limits of your abilities and when to call for help. Keep a first aid kit in your bag (as I covered in detail earlier in Packing Your Bags) and know any national or local numbers for emergency services besides 911. If you do have a first aid situation, ask the class if there is anyone more qualified than you to administer first aid. You may have a doctor or nurse in your class. You might be worried about what is expected of you and whether your help could cause more injury or lead to a lawsuit. Most countries have a simple law saying that first aid, done with good intention, is protected from that kind of problem. If in doubt, use the wisdom of others around you, but don't be afraid to try and help. As a belly dance teacher you shouldn't have the responsibility of first aid, unless it's a condition of your employment. Make it clear when administering first aid that you do so as a friend and not in any qualified position. I have taught over four thousand lessons and (knock on wood) have never had to do more than offer bandages for blisters. I hope your experience is similar.

Avoid physical injuries by starting each lesson with a good warm-up and asking latecomers to warm up to one side before joining in with the class. Watch for student fatigue when drilling any move or combination, and move on to the next activity when they seem to lose focus. Work both sides of the body in turn and start all moves at a medium tempo. Repeating moves at a fast pace for too long can affect balance, coordination, and focus. Repeating moves very slowly for a long time can cause muscle fatigue and overstretching. Mix your tempos, body parts, and sides regularly to keep things interesting and avoid stress on any one part of the body.

Include a request for information about the students' current and long-term health in your waiver, and remind your students to update their waiver should their health change over the course of their study with you.

Finally, take out insurance. The initial outlay could save you millions in the long term. There is more information about insurance later in the book.

KEEPING PERFORMERS SAFE

The position of teacher also quickly develops into troupe director as you find opportunities for your students to perform outside of the classroom setting. Sad to say, our dance is often linked in the mind of the public with stripping or adult entertainment or something seductive performed for our partners. (Of course, we know that it is far from seductive for our poor partners to watch us drill or practice choreography, be that in the bedroom, kitchen, or garage.) Until this public perception changes, we need to continue to educate, through both our words and our actions, and keep ourselves and our students safe from insults and propositions.

There are a few fairly simple steps we can take to keep ourselves and our baby dancers safe:

Don't let audience members touch you inappropriately — In some areas body tipping is the expected norm, but if you don't like this you can change the norm. If you are OK with body tipping, then offer up the side of your hip. It is hard for audiences to understand complex tipping etiquette, so have your rules nice and clear, then stick to them. Ask yourself how much you need that $1 bill!

Don't let audience members hold your hand for too long — It is often necessary to take their hand to encourage them to leave their seat, but do you keep holding their hand once they are up dancing? Do you hold both of their hands so that you dance exclusively for that one person? How about letting them lead you? Twirl you? Stand behind you with their hands on your hips? As performers, we need to focus our attention at the room as a whole, rather than become one person's special dancer. Dance is one long conversation spoken in body language. Dancers need to be careful with what they say and what others understand. It is perfectly possible to be warm, friendly, and welcoming and yet remain a mysterious, aloof fantasy.

Teach your students the belly dancer hustle — It is that special dance of avoiding wandering hands and overly enthusiastic party dancers and getting stuck by one table for too long. Teach them to never turn their back on anyone, to rescue their dance sisters from sticky spots, and to be aware of the whole room while making the birthday guest feel special. Most important, they need to do all this while smiling, looking relaxed, and dancing beautifully.

Become a member of the family — In restaurant work, the waiting and managing staff can be your best protection or your worst nightmare. If they consider you part of their family, then they will protect you like a sister or brother. If they don't respect you, neither will the audience. Focus on building the management's respect from the start by not undercutting their current dancer and by arriving to check out the venue smartly dressed and on time. It can help your cause no end to bring along a man or older lady with you when you interview. I know it may be vexing to have to do so in this day and age, but that escort may signal the management that you are respected and cared for. Of course, it also helps keep you safe. Explain your tipping requests to the management and clarify what time you will be performing. If you can, get all the details down in an email or written contract. Make it clear what time you will be leaving and how much "everyone up to dance" time you are willing to give. If they offer you a meal as part of your payment, then ask if there is a quiet corner away from the party where you can eat.

Dress to impress — Sometimes you will need to arrive and leave in costume, but use your clothing as a clear indication of when you are on and off duty. Arrive in a coat or cover-up; otherwise, your music may just start up as you enter the room. Once you have completed your paid "everyone up to dance" time, leave the dance floor and put your cover-up on to collect your payment, eat your food, or head off to your next job. Sometimes you will want to stay and enjoy the party; perhaps you have friends at the restaurant or you love the atmosphere. It is still important to take your time to shake off the belly dancer persona and introduce the room to your real self. Get changed, remove your bling, and do something different with your hair; otherwise, the audience will think you are still the belly dancer and demand more entertainment from you. The event organizer might ask why they pay you to pull everyone up on the dance floor if it's something you are willing to do for free.

Keep your distance — Beware of customers and managers who want to introduce you to their friends. It can be a wonderful feeling to be the center of attention and in high demand, but realize that it is not you they like but your belly dancer persona. You may find that conversation soon dries up, as the friend laps up the feeling of being in the company of a beautiful belly dancer and forgets to talk. If they offer you the chance to star in their movie, dance in their restaurant, or meet their pop star boss, politely take their card and move on. I did once teach a film star to dance. They contacted me via my website, and I was so used to hearing this same spiel that I ignored it until I got a frantic phone call from the star's mother. If they want you, they will find a way to book you.

Don't be caught alone — Avoid allowing yourself to be separated from the herd. Take a dresser or driver with you to gigs so that no one needs to offer to walk you to your car. Don't step outside to share a cigarette with someone or to take a phone call. Don't accept a lift from strangers or offer to take someone on to the next venue. Don't go to their home to meet their mother, or invite them to your house to fix your dishwasher. Don't offer private lessons in your home unless someone else will be there. If you don't have someone, invent a friend who will be picking you up in ten minutes.

Don't date audience members.

168

Why do we have to be so cautious? What puts belly dancers in greater danger than other performers? Simply put, a percentage of our audience still thinks we are prostitutes. This may be because of the way we dance, or the way we dress, the fact that we are out late at night without a man, or a cultural perception. Of course a lady should be able to do these things without being seen as a prostitute, but it may take more than a generation to change that perception, and while we wait for it to change or work on educating the public, we have to live with it in some form and educate our students in the reality of being a working belly dancer.

You can't necessarily spot him, but be on the lookout for a dangerous man or two in every room. Let me give you a quick look into that man's mind. His father was stationed in the Middle East when he was a boy, and he believes that "belly dancer" in Arabic/army slang means prostitute. In his teens he read a book in which the belly dancer seduced a man with her dance of the seven veils, and belly dancers appear in his porn collection. Before coming out tonight, he sent a video clip of a belly dancer shaking her bootie around her bedroom to all his friends. They have been drinking. A girl who looks a lot like you has been sending him topless photos through his dating site. He noticed you when you arrived with too much makeup on and a short skirt like the whores on the street wear. Then you did this really naughty dance and gave him the eye. He bought you for $20 that you let him slip into your bra, and then he bought you a drink when you asked the manager to introduce you to his table. All his friends have seen how you are looking at him. He has the hottest girl in the room laughing at his jokes and leaning forward so he can see cleavage, inviting him to add another $20. He asks to see you again, and you say you will be here this time next week. He asks to see you sooner and you say you are busy, but you laugh as you say it. He asks for your number, and you give him your card. Now if you ask him to carry your bags to your car, he hears something completely different.

This may seem to do a huge disservice to the many wonderful men who come to belly dance shows, but I am simply trying to convince you that part of being a belly dancer is knowing how to stay friendly and entertaining while also being untouchable. Put yourself and your dancers behind glass like a museum treasure, to be looked at and admired but never touched or broken.

KEEPING YOURSELF SAFE

Even as a teacher you need to be aware of your surroundings. Carrying a heavy bag out to a dark parking lot is a classic situation to make you feel vulnerable, but don't forget about paying attention when you let yourself into your venue or when you tidy up at the end of your lesson. There's safety in numbers; if you can, ask a student to walk with you to your car or the bus stop.

Belly dance teachers also seem to be particularly susceptible to stalkers both online and off. Be aware of who you link up with on social media, and don't take a mutual friend as a sign that you should accept a stranger's request. It is fairly easy to do an image search online to check whether someone is a "catfish"; that is, someone who hides behind a fake name and photograph to get close to you. I suggest you establish a work social network site in addition to your personal one, or set up a fan page, so that you can keep some business distance between you and your students. It is fine to Like someone's kitten pictures, but before joining in a conversation, ask yourself whether this is someone you'd want to meet face-to-face after class. Avoid joining conversations about politics, religion, money, or relationships if you feel they may affect your business or lose you students.

Once you become a popular teacher, it is only natural that you start to have students who come to multiple classes per week, but watch out for the ones who seem overly interested in you as a person or who ask personal questions. If you have any worries about an overly affectionate or needy student, share your thoughts with others – say, your boss or a fellow teacher – but resist the temptation to talk about it with any of your students. Sadly, a lot of people have an emptiness in part of their lives, and we have all seen the joy that belly dance can bring when it fills the gap. Dancers can learn to love their bodies, to trust their instincts, to become graceful, powerful, strong, and fit. Being able to share that journey with our students is a wonderful side effect of teaching them belly dance, one you will enjoy. However, transforming part of their life does not qualify a teacher as a guru or as any more of a wise woman than anyone else. When students turn to you to answer other life questions they have or to fill in other gaps in their lives, you will disappoint them. Don't step over into the realm of therapist unless you are qualified; even then, I feel that doing so will change your belly dance teaching experience. Suddenly withdrawing your support or being revealed as fallible may break the spell of how this person sees you and stir up anger. If this happens to you, make it clear that you won't have any further conversations with that person, either online or off, without someone else present. Keep your boss or another teacher informed about the situation. There is no rule in teaching belly dance that says you have to teach someone who makes you feel uncomfortable or afraid. The person making you uncomfortable should have a support group of family, doctors, teachers, and friends who are better able than you to offer understanding and help.

Once you begin teaching belly dance, your body becomes your tools of the trade, and as such, it deserves extra care. A broken leg is very inconvenient but tolerable at a desk job; for you it could mean months without work.

Here are three fundamental practices for keeping your essential tools in good working order:

- Before class, eat some good protein and drink water.

- Allow time to arrive early at your venues so that you don't have to move furniture or sweep the floor in a rush.

- Set up, and stick to, a weekly plan for moderate workouts that complement belly dance, such as yoga, swimming, or Pilates, and balance that with activities you love that keep you fit and healthy.

Belly dance teachers also need to be wary of showing students how not to do a move and thus injuring themselves. Use your hands to sketch a motion rather than testing your vulnerable joints. If you teach multiple lessons in a week, be aware of over drilling your body if the same moves or combinations come up in lesson after lesson. Offset your start dates or write a slightly different term plan for each class, so you can focus on upper and lower body, hip lifts and drops, and stationary and travelling moves to balance out your week of work and the stresses on your body.

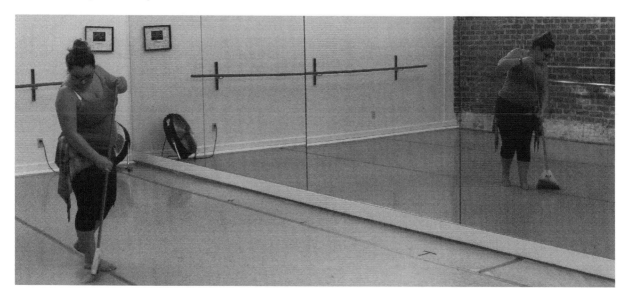

TAKING IT FURTHER: HAFLA AND OTHER FUN STUFF!

Once your students have been dancing for a while, it is great to introduce them to the idea of performance and to give them some opportunities to perform. Right from the start I like to invite them to come and see me dance, to attend hafla and stage shows. I post on social network sites, prepare an events handout, and talk about my performances in class. It may take a little while for your students to actually come to one, but don't be disheartened. It is very brave of people to come out to an unfamiliar restaurant or a show on their own. They may well ask their sister or a friend to go with them, but if they don't like the idea or it's a difficult time, your students may not feel able to walk into a new situation without the support of someone else. If you can, try to be that support. Maybe offer to meet beforehand to carpool or try to gather a large group together. Once a small group has been to see you dance, they will sell it to your other students for you.

The safest and easiest place to start your students performing is in your own dance space. Allocate the last half hour of a class, perhaps the last one of a course, and perform for each other. If your beginner group has learned choreography, split the group into two so that each person can perform it once and watch it once. Divide your most confident students between the two groups, so that both are equally skilled. Then it's a good idea to dance a number or two yourself, but keep the numbers short and upbeat. Maybe show them the choreography you plan to teach in the next course (this may also encourage them to rebook) or a prop you hope they will learn to use. If you have students who have been coming for a while, they may want to perform last year's choreography or a solo of their own. Ask the group if they are willing to attend the end-of-course party at one of your other classes and perform for them. Once this pattern becomes established, you will find that dancers are quietly preparing solos, duets, and small group numbers with an eye to these end-of-term gatherings.

After a few of these you may feel your students are ready for the real world. Many dance communities organize events to showcase dancers of different levels. If you are new to the area, make a point of attending some of these to check out which are friendly and what the expectations are. It is not fair to take your beginners to a showcase that features only professional dancers, even if they market themselves as open to all.

Once you have found the perfect venue, pick a date at least ten weeks ahead, to give every-one time to prepare, with both their dancing and their stage nerves. Add the date to your handouts and start talking about the performance in general terms in each class. In my class introduction, I mention the date and offer the idea that those who want to can perform. It is totally normal at this stage for everyone to look panicked. Be clear that no one will be forced to perform, but belly dance is a performance art and it is good to work toward performance as a goal. Each time we practice the choreography I remind them why we keep rehearsing and the date of our performance.

About a month before the performance, someone will ask about costumes, or you can bring it up yourself. Either way, that will give you a good gauge of how many of them are really thinking about performing. Write up a couple of good-quality handouts (see the suggestions that follow) and run through them during class time, taking questions. Be reassuring and confident. A few weeks before the performance, move them away from the mirrors so you can judge who knows the dance and who is following someone else. This also helps them under-stand that the dance stage will be different from their practice room. Stop using terms such as "turn to the door" and make sure they can perform without any cues from you, verbal or nonverbal. Plan the week before the performance to be a dress rehearsal, and no matter what their ability is at that time, praise them highly. In the theater directors tend to rant during the dress rehearsal in the belief that by crushing the actors they will get a better performance. I don't think that works with belly dance. If you have prepared the dancers, taught them about performance skills as well as the choreography, and picked a good venue, then they should be ready.

I present some examples of handouts for preparing to perform later in the book; here are a few of my favorites:

Choreography Handout — Details of the dance plus a shorter version with key words or phrases. Don't forget to date and include all details such as music artist(s) and your copyright.

Venue Handout — Map and directions to the venue, parking options, and which door to use. You may want to add details about the seating, food, restrooms, and changing areas.

Packing list — I suggest you ask dancers to pack in a suitcase or a flight bag on wheels. It's a good idea to use a larger bag than you actually need, so that you can find an earring at the bottom without having to empty the whole bag onto the floor. If you have a dozen ladies all with blue skirts, it is hard to identify whose they are unless the dancers keep them in the bags as much as possible. The packing list should include all parts of the costume, underwear, cover-up, makeup, jewelry, music, props, safety pins, toupee tape, dab-on perfume, after-party clothes, map, directions, a charged-up camera, and a small purse (if you are minding everyone's purses, you will be grateful if they all fit into one larger bag; a backpack is ideal).

Timeline Handout — This is a useful exercise for any dancer, but is essential for someone new to performing. It can be as simple as a table for the dancers themselves to fill in, but for your first-timers, it's wise to do all the preparation for them. Work backward from the performance time and give an estimate of the time it will take to travel, pack bags, do makeup and hair, shower, and eat. Also list the work that needs to be done in the days before – such as a last rehearsal, painting nails, and checking the route – all the way back to three weeks before, when we want them to ask their friends to attend.

Behavior Handout — I usually call this "How to be a belly dancer" or something similar, but it covers the behavior that I expect. It is hard to know in advance how your students will behave outside the class rooms setting. They could be intimidated by all the attention – or encouraged to act inappropriately. Of course, you cannot be expected to be their mother, but they are representing you as a teacher, and it will reflect badly on you if they get drunk and dance naked on the tables. My theory is that by setting out clear and rather conservative rules I can allow them to all feel safe and bend the rules a little while also knowing the standards I expect. Obviously it is important that you also stick with your rules and lead by example. Should you feel your group needs to let off steam after a performance, you can always move on to a new venue or ask your dancers to change after the performance and then let them go "off duty." If they will get to watch the rest of the show, take time beforehand to tell them how to be a good audience member, how to interact with the other dancers, what kind of applause or cheering is expected, and what the local tipping etiquette involves.

Performer's Contract — This contract is to avoid any misunderstandings about their responsibilities, your responsibilities, and any money involved. We teachers know how the belly dance world works; students without performance experience don't know any of this. (I heard of a new dancer who went to the dance studio about half an hour before her first performance elsewhere, because she assumed that her teacher would have organized taxis to the venue for everyone!) Be clear about who pays for the costumes, transportation, and entry fee to the venue. Decide how to share any tips and also be clear about payment. Usually student troupes don't receive any payment, but sometimes a venue will pay the teacher for bringing in lots of customers. If you try to keep this kind of information from your students, they will find out. Tell them that you are going to use that payment to cover the meal and a round of drinks, or to buy a welcome mat for the studio, or to start off the tipping. Work out what happens if someone has to cancel and how you can limit that damage. Also, be clear about the intellectual rights: who owns any photographs and video taken during the event, where they can be shared, and whether anyone is getting a payment from them. Sometimes it is worth having a professional photographer at an event; dancers may be happy to purchase a better than average photo of themselves.

Costume Handout —A picture and instructions about the costume you want them to wear (see details in the next section, "Picking Out a Group Costume"). Don't forget underwear (don't risk getting a reputation as "that" teacher), makeup, and jewelry. You may also want them to purchase and maintain a prop and a cover-up.

PICKING OUT A GROUP COSTUME

When picking a costume for your group, think back to how you felt when you first started dancing. Most people are not used to showing a lot of flesh, and each person in your group will have a list of areas she doesn't want to show. This can be really limiting, leaving almost no other costume choice but a full cover-up. At this early point in your students' dance journey, the costume is less important than giving them the confidence to get up on stage, so tend toward compromise. Allowing them a safe, affordable, and comfortable costume also helps to market them to the audience as beginner dancers, and audiences tend to be very supportive and forgiving of beginner belly dancers.

Try to think of cheap ways to dress up items they already have or to make easy purchases. Look in shops for T-shirts or tank tops with an Arabic feel, a keyhole neck, sequins or sparkle. If you do want to buy off the rack, factor in cost and also the size range.
Most dancers have a pair of yoga-style black pants; if you add a coin belt, you have a very basic uniform style costume.

For a saiidi or folkloric style number, you may be able to find a full-length, square-cut shift dress. If you are looking for a more layered look, then bring in some of your collection to help your students shop wisely.

A group costume has to be either all one style or all one color, and the overall look needs to be as if everyone visited the same shop with the same budget. Nothing looks sadder than three ladies in off-the-rack dresses and one in a thousand-dollar bedlah.

Covering a bra is not as difficult as it first may seem, especially if you can chose fabric that stands on its own and doesn't need embellishment for a simple, student troupe look. Providing your group with an order code for fabric allows them to set their own budget, use pieces they already have, and tweak their design to suit their body shape.

Beware of trying to talk your students into expensive costumes early on. Some traders will give you a credit if your students spend money with them, but in the long term your students will question your motives and wonder whether you always have their best interests at heart. If you do want to take advantage of this kind of offer, tell your students and maybe offer to spend your commission on matching veils for the group.

You may have a student who really wants to wear a costume she has already purchased. I explain that I like to keep the group in matching outfits and then offer her the chance to develop a solo to match her costume in the future.

Helping your group choose a costume can be stressful, as you struggle to negotiate everyone's wishes, but they look to you for leadership, so consider all options, hear everyone out, and then make a clear and final decision early on.

ORGANIZING YOUR OWN EVENT

Sometimes there is nowhere around to perform with your group, so you need to organize your own event to showcase your students. I strongly suggest you start off small, as events can quickly swamp you with logistics. First run a small student night, work your way up to a hafla, organize a workshop, and then maybe move on to a dance day or stage show.

STUDENT NIGHT

This is a simple gathering of your students to dance with each other, not dissimilar from an end-of-course party. Pick a venue that your group will fill, such as someone's home or a restaurant, or hire a room. Check whether your insurance will cover this as an end-of-term party or if you need to get events insurance. Ask everyone to bring a dish or commit to a set menu. Invite your students ahead of time to perform, and let them know that you'll get music selections from them a few weeks in advance so that you can prepare a playlist and running order. If the class has learned choreography, you may have to let a soloist, duets, and trios perform the same number, splitting them up in the running order with different numbers. Set a performance time and ask everyone to be on site thirty to forty-five minutes ahead of that to socialize. Check whether your music system will play loudly enough to fill the space; if not, buy or rent a set of speakers.

You should be able to compare and stage manage this size event by yourself, but designate someone to play the music, someone else to take photos, and another person to manage the door if you are taking an entry fee. At these events dancers will be happy to change in a restroom, bedroom, or bathroom and keep their bags with them. Ask all those performing to bring friends and family to make up the audience. The fee for this kind of event will depend on the food, but try to keep it as low as possible to still cover your costs.

At a student night I like to let all the dancers sit and watch the whole show; I simply call people up from the audience to perform. I allow anyone to perform almost anything at these kinds of events. You may have a dislike of 1970s pop, but if it inspires your students and gets them thinking about writing choreography, working together, and performing, then it can be part of the learning process. My only restrictions tend to be that all performances must be suitable for a family audience. Tiny costumes and bad language don't go down very well in most settings.

HAFLA

Once you have organized a few student nights it may be time to move on to a hafla. This Middle Eastern style dance party takes on a different flavor depending on where in the world you are, but it's your party and you can set the tone to suit your group. Start planning a hafla about three months ahead by picking a venue and date. List your dates on a few prominent websites so as not to have someone else local organize a similar event on the same date, and set up an events page on a few social network sites.

Your venue can still be a hall, house, or restaurant, or you may want to approach hotels or an outside venue. Be creative, but keep an eye on the price. To determine a ticket price, do some quick calculations of what your costs may be and divide that by your expected audience. Add a little wiggle room for unexpected expenses or a smaller-than-expected crowd.

You may want to pay a belly dancer you admire to perform at your hafla as the star of the show, or another local teacher may be willing to bring her students, but expect to pay her gas money.

It is still acceptable to ask the audience to bring a dish to share, or your venue may want to provide food (that the audience will pay for) in return for a discount on the venue hire. Decide whether you want a bar and whether it will be an open or a no-host bar. I suggest that you don't include the price of drinks with your ticket price. This encourages performers to drink early in the evening before the bar runs dry, and it changes the tone of the event. Be aware that outside bars may be hesitant to take a belly dance event because we tend to not be heavy drinkers or spend on the more expensive alcoholic drinks. I think it is fair to warn them that the evening will be mostly ladies and soft drinks, so that they have the chance to bring mixers for nonalcoholic cocktails, which will push up their profits.

You will need plenty of volunteers to help with your hafla. In addition to a photographer, DJ, and door host, you may want to ask someone else to MC; find a stage manager too, and you'll be freed up to oversee the whole evening. Allocate volunteers to areas – such as the changing rooms, lobby, food area, and seating – and ask them to take full charge, from setup to clearing. Send them detailed notes beforehand of how you want the room set up, performers' rules, and where to store money. You may also want to invite stall holders or run a raffle, and these areas need volunteer managers too.

The more information you give your helpers beforehand, the less stressful your event will be. Don't sweat the small stuff; let others make decisions. I recall that at one event the whole room was set up mirror image to my vision, but it ran beautifully and everyone had a great night.

Set up a box of stationery that everyone can help themselves to, with string and push pins, stickers and index cards, extra raffle tickets, small notepads, and pens of every style. You never know what might be important for your helpers, so have everything they could possibly need. Keep all your helpers' job descriptions in that box so they can swap jobs in a hurry without bothering you. Ask someone to be in charge of any money on the night, and give them a notebook and starting cash for change. They will need to remove cash from the front door and raffle area at regular intervals throughout the event. Make sure the helpers in those areas know the system so that money can be put safely away without too much fuss. Ask someone qualified to be the event first aider, and make sure all the other volunteers know who that is. You may also want someone to be guest star liaison and an assistant for yourself.

It is fair to offer a free ticket or a discounted price for all the volunteers, although first aiders shouldn't be charged because there is always a chance that they may have to leave the venue or miss part of the show to attend to an injury.

You will need event insurance, and you may need permission to play music. Your venue should be able to clarify those details with you, or you could seek legal advice. Ask all your performers to sign a waiver form and send them clear instructions on what is expected of them. Your waiver may exclude you from any responsibility should they injure themselves, in addition to stating that you have no control over any photographs or reviews of the event that may end up in press or online. You should also prepare them a contract with all the details of time, place, and venue type and limitations on their performance length, style, and suitability.

Think about how much you want to perform, and set yourself some limits so that you don't spread your energy too thin. It may be better for you to open the show than close it, meaning you can arrive at the venue ready to perform and then be available for troubleshooting for most of the evening. I don't perform with any of my class groups, because that could mean that I would spend the whole night changing from one costume to the next while also running the event, perhaps holding up the show and stressing the already-nervous students. It is better to find yourself a spot at the back of the room and watch the show where anyone who wants you can easily find you.

Book the room for at least an hour before paying customers arrive for setup and for an hour after the show for clearing out. You may be expected to leave the venue as you found it, so pack cleaning products.

My packing list includes:

- Toilet paper, tissues, liquid soap
- Underskirts, spare coin belts, veils, finger cymbals, sticks, wrap tops for lending to performers who have a costume or prop malfunction
- Safety pins, double sided tape or toupee tape, sewing kit for running repairs
- Hair bands, flowers, clips, and hair spray
- Cleaning wet wipes, floor cloth, air freshener, hand broom and pan
- Phone, camera, all relevant emails, all ticket sales, all dancers' contracts, spare waivers, paperwork
- Calculator, cash box, and stationery box
- Handouts for volunteers
- Printed signs (No Exit, Stage Entrance, Performers Changing Room, No Smoking), with low-tack tape and pushpins
- Bag of veils or tablecloths for backdrop, table covers, curtains
- Water and food for myself
- My costumes, evening dress, cover-up, cleaning clothes

The more preparation you do ahead of time, the more smoothly your event will run, so don't be afraid to set a deadline for ticket purchases and for information from your performers. If I don't have a limit on the number of tickets I can sell, then my deadline is always the night before, so we don't have to make sales at the door, which can be an added stress. I have always had cash as well as online payments arriving up until midnight the night before, so be prepared: put on a little makeup and wear street clothes in case the doorbell rings.

Collecting music and information from the dancers a week or two before the event gives you the chance to make sure these work on your player, fit in with the guidelines, and enable you to plan a balanced running order. Audiences love to know the title of the music or more about the style of each dancer, so put a program at the front door or on each table. You can also include the website for each dancer or some information about the music artist.
For some reason it is unusual in the belly dance world to ask performers to commit to a piece of music ahead of time, but this can result in two people turning up with the same CD, or a show that is dominated by one music artist or dance style. Most performers are practicing their performance a week or so before and are happy to send the music if asked, giving you a few days to work out a balanced show.

WORKSHOPS

Workshops are a wonderful way to introduce your students to new teaching styles and topics that you may not normally teach. Unfortunately, it is very hard for workshop organizers to make any kind of profit from workshops unless they live in an area where the prices are high and the competition is low. Most teachers organize workshops because they want their students to have the opportunity to study with another teacher, and they see a discounted or free ticket as the only payment needed for all the hard work. Your costs for a workshop are going to be fairly simple:

- Venue rental
- Teacher fee and travel expenses
- Insurance
- Admin (phone calls, printed tickets, flyers)
- Advertising
- Water, tea, coffee, snacks, and serving items.

Estimate the number of people attending and divide your costs by that number. Some workshop teachers may take a sliding scale or a 60/40 split, which can help if you are unsure of how many people you can get to attend. Set a level for the workshop (beginner, intermediate or advance) and send invites out to everyone you want to be there. It's a good idea to create an event on social network sites and make a simple flyer to distribute at local events. Make sure your flyer is neat, clear and contains all the information, including how to register. If you are on good terms with other local teachers, they may be happy for you to mail them a dozen flyers for them to hand out in class.

Think about the best way to use your workshop teacher's time; a lower-level workshop may attract more dancers, or advanced dancers may pay more for a tough topic or smaller groups.

Often big-name dancers who are in town for a weekend event will be happy to teach a smaller weekday workshop for a smaller fee and the chance to see the sights or to get some home-cooked food. Be mindful not to step on the toes of the organizers of the big events, but if you can fill an empty day or offer an overnight along their journey, they may appreciate the invitation. If you already have a strong class and a nice venue, look at simply extending your venue booking and keeping everything simple.

On the day of the workshop, you will need to check payments and make sure the event runs on schedule. Dancers love to have group photos from their workshops, so be sure to bring a camera. Make sure your teacher knows the timing and can see a clock. Again, a short contract or detailed email can clarify what is expected from both the organizer and the workshop teacher. As the organizer it is your role to make the workshop teacher look good, so provide water, the music player, and photocopies of handouts, and politely keep the teacher informed of the time.

DAY OF DANCE

A day of dance is a combination of a workshop or two with a hafla. They are popular with organizers, as the hafla should make a profit that will balance out any loss from the workshop. This means that they can take more gambles with less-well-known teachers or unusual topics. Organizing a big event like this can take a lot of planning and works best with a team of help ers with clearly defined roles.

Plan the day with a variety of different customers in mind. Your beginner dancers may want to attend only one workshop, and if that workshop is toward the end of the day they are more likely to stay on to see the show. An advanced workshop in the mix will encourage profession-al dancers to book. Look also at workshops that are slightly more outside the box: makeup, costuming, drumming, and photography workshops may appeal to the family, friends, and partners of your usual students.

STAGE SHOW

These may look like the ultimate glamorous event, but of course all that grace on stage takes a huge amount of direction behind the scenes.

In addition to the usual helpers, you will need a crew of runners for your stage manager, lighting and sound techs, and a dresser or dressing room manager. You might also want to ask someone to take on the task of promoting ticket sales through local news, radio, and social media.

Make sure your insurance covers you outside of class time and that the venue you are using has building insurance. You may have to make it clear whether your event is public or private. For example, your homeowner's insurance will probably cover you if you invite your friends over for a party in your garden, but not if you advertise it as a show and charge guests at the door. If in doubt, get yourself some separate events insurance. Insurance companies offer policies for twelve months of insurance with a maximum number of events and a maximum number of attendees. You can save yourself some money if you think ahead when you plan to hold your events. If you like to hold them at Christmas, March, May, and September, think about getting your insurance to cover you from the last week in May and then running next year's event earlier in May so you can cover five events with one premium payment. Then hold off on renewing until just before your September event and do the same thing again.

It is useful to make clear to your stage show performers the behavior you expect and the type of performance you would like to see. It is not unusual now to have a contract or written request that clarifies these elements. Decide whether your event will be open to all, including men and children. Are you going to pay dancers to perform? Can you help them with their travel costs? Do performers have to pay or buy food? If you don't expect performers to pay, where will the income come from? What time do performers have to arrive? Do you need music beforehand? On disk or as downloaded or emailed files? Do they have to commit to music ahead of time, or can they just turn up and perform? Do you want fusion, tribal, or only classical? Can they dance to jazz or rock or punk? How long can their music be? Can they include political statements, sexual content, or comedy in their routine? How much flesh can they show? What quality of costume will you accept? And do you want them to stay in costume for a finale? Can they video their performance, or are you going to do that for them?

It is best to write a long letter or email making all these things clear. Performers don't mind being told what you expect in a nice friendly letter, but they do get upset if you don't tell them, and then on the night of the show you are offended or an assumption causes an upset.
An example of a performer's contract is available at the back of this book.

RUNNING ORDER

In the realm of belly dance, the running order – that is, the schedule of acts in the show – forms a minefield of unwritten social etiquette that you can learn only through hard experience; some of these rules are still mystifying to veteran performers. They are the equivalent of wedding seating plans, and if you want to master them, you are well advised to stock up on a supply of scrap paper, sticky notes, and a suit of armor.

Here are a few of the rules of running orders:

- Age after beauty. Dancers with a long dance history go on later in the show.
- Students before teachers. A teacher cannot dance until all her students have performed. This may be very complicated to follow if students study with lots of local teachers.
- Nerves before confidence. Allow anyone performing for the first time to go on early in the show.
- Split up the styles. If you have five ATS groups and five classical solos, then they will run better alternately.
- Experts after the lighthearted. A deeply researched folkloric dance should go after the funny pop song.
- Save your best until last. The great dancers go on later. You may rate your dancers by experience or by how much the audience loves them.
- Keep them guessing. Mix up the styles, groups and solos, costume colors and tempo.
- Don't forget the costume changes. If someone is performing more than once they need at least two numbers as changing times.

You may notice that obeying all of these rules will cause so much confusion that it is impossible to please everyone. Pick one or two rules that you think are important to your particular event and focus on those.

There are four key slots to fill in the average show:

- First half opening
- First half closing
- Second half opening
- Second half closing

Your star of the show takes the second half closing slot. She will expect it and so will your audience. In my opinion, your second guest star should either take the closing of the first half or dance second to last in the second half.

The opening slots for each half need upbeat numbers and confident dancers to set the tone and warm up the audience. These spots tend to be unpopular because warming up an audience is hard work, and the dancers may have to perform for a minute or two over chatter or polite applause. I like to take one of these myself so that I can prepare while still being available to manage the event. You might also give one to a young upcoming star or a group with a really upbeat number.

Emotional dances seem to work best when they go third or forth in either half. I am not sure why, but musicals also follow that formula, so perhaps it is unconsciously natural for the audience to want some substance at that point in a show.

With these important slots taken, you can start to fill in the gaps with your least experienced dancers, working from there toward your more confident dancers and with an eye to keeping the show balanced and interesting.

As soon as your running list is finalized, you will hear about a dancer who really wants to perform and another who regretfully can't make it. Then you find yourself rewriting your running order. It is a good idea to have a strong plan in place a week or so before the event, but to be flexible enough to make changes right up until the end of your show.

Exercise - Plan a running order for these performers:

__ Yourself, dancing your favorite solo
__ A group of older ladies, dancing to 1990's pop
__ Their teacher, who usually does something light and funny
__ A group of teens who are dancing to classical Egyptian
__ Their teacher, who wants to dance Saiidi. She is also in the Egyptian number above
__ A young and upcoming dancer who usually does something dark and gothic
__ A very theatrical dancer in her fifties who has not been dancing long but is a famous actress; she has a long nay taqsim
__ Your teacher
__ Your teacher's mentor
__ Your local ATS group
__ An ATS duet from their ranks – two dancers who are less skilled than the group as a whole
__ A local teacher who always entertains the audience but doesn't seem to use many belly dance moves and doesn't use belly dance music
__ A young dancer who dances Turkish-tribal fusion and never, ever smiles
__ A friend of yours who danced belly dance in a top restaurant forty years ago but now performs only once or twice a year
__ A mother-and-daughter duet who have told you their dance is Turkish, but whose music has a strong Spanish flavor

There is no right or wrong for this exercise, but it is a good experiment. Next time you go to a show, take a look at the running order when you arrive and see how you would have planned it differently. After the show, note what worked and what didn't. Would your running order have been better?

MEET YOUR CLASS

Now that you are ready to start teaching your class, I thought it might be useful to take a lighthearted look at some of the amazing students you may meet in the course of your journey and some of the issues and challenges they may bring. This list is not exclusive, and my aim is not to offend, but to help you as a teacher prepare for both the best, the worst, and the most baffling. I have tried to use gender-neutral names, as many of these could be male or female students, and the names used bear no relationship to any of my previous students. All of us have displayed some of these personality traits at some point. These are not based on individual students; they are a blend of memorable characteristics of some of the dancers I have met over the years. Enjoy!

Alex will be the first person to contact you when your website goes live, your flyers go up, or you post your classes on a social network site. She will write you a long and gushing email about how excited she is, or she will ring one evening to tell you about the coin belt she has bought and the DVD she has been studying. She will never come to class. She is busy ringing the salsa dance teacher and ordering her salsa fit DVD.

Bailey saw your advert then called or emailed to give you some advice. She thinks that Tuesday nights will suit more people than Wednesdays. Six p.m. is a little early, in her opinion, and the hall you have chosen is not as good as the hall nearer her house. She is there on night one, but continues this conversation for the next fifteen years, helpfully bringing in flyers for new halls or dance studios.

Casey and her twenty-seven friends would all love to come to class tomorrow. You ask your dance studio if you can move into the larger room; to be ready, you print out thirty handouts. Casey and her group do not show up.

Dale would like you to dance or teach for free at her gallery opening/women's drum circle/ school festival/high school reunion. She doesn't want to pay, because it will be good exposure for you; she is positive you will get dozens of new students. You never get a single new student from these events. Ask for cash.

Emery will be a regular from the beginning, attending every week, working hard, and getting on well with the others. She will perform once or twice at small events and will buy a couple of nice costumes. One day you notice that Emery has not been in for a few weeks. The weeks turn into years. You keep her on your mailing list, but she disappears from your social network site and never replies to your emails. Ten years later she appears in class. You ask her how she has been. She says "Fine." You may never know what happened. If she does want to tell you, she probably left her husband, moved around the world, had three kids, got into politics and has moved home to be mayor. But she just wants to dance.

Finn has a secret. Whatever it is, she doesn't want to share it with the group. She doesn't want to talk about her job, her love life, or anything else. She comes to class every week and loves it in her very reserved way. You are her dance teacher, and there is nothing you can do unless you see bruises. Let her have her hour of fun each week.

Gray shares too much. Within ten minutes your whole class will know the placement of all her piercings and her preferences in underwear. The phrase "And back to the belly dancing!" comes in handy when dealing with her.

Harper arrives late with three shopping bags, a coat, and a bunch of flowers. During class she turns the wrong way, asks for things to be explained again and again, will probably make notes and stand on her skirt. She will never have a veil, and the other students don't want to be her partner in case they get stepped on. Yet if you give her time, Harper will turn into one of your best dancers. She is clumsy because she cares and she is thinking about every move in

many different ways at the same time. She may dance at a much more emotional level than the others. She will stick with you forever because she understands that belly dance is not a subject she can master in six months. Invest a little more time and let her know you understand her. Also, rotate partners frequently so everyone gets the chance to work with her.

Ira just got back from Egypt. She has photos of her bathroom, which is gold and turquoise and has pyramids drawn on the ceiling. She will be a very popular member of your group because she makes amazing baklava and brings everyone back costumes from her trips. She isn't bothered about the dancing, so let her tell tales from the Nile while you all knock out a five-minute shimmy.

Jemm will ring or email to ask if you take male students. I hope you say yes. He wants to know about the changing rooms, any difficulties, if the other students will let him join. Send him lots of information and tell him he is going to be most welcome. Jemm may never feel able to attend class. He is very nervous and thinks he won't be accepted. If you can tell him about your other male students, an upcoming show with a male performer, or another local class with male students, you may be able to lure him in.

Kendall is grumpy because a woman at work told him he is sexist. He thinks you are sexist for running female-only dance classes. His email will seem odd. Answer Kendall the same way you answered Jemm. He will reply "But I am a MAN!" Make sure he feels welcome and then leave him alone. He will never come to class.

London has been coming to shows for a while as a spouse or a photographer or a drummer, but you have seen him secretly hip dropping at the bar. Tell him that one day you want him to come to your class. Put him on the mailing list and make sure he knows about any free lessons. You may be able to use him to meet Jemm. If you can get him into a class, he will stay forever, work hard and become a key member of your group.

Mattie likes to learn everything from the feet up. She will make you stop and think about the exact point where your weight shifts as you cross the floor and which way your toes are pointing. She will be very good for your dancing but also hard to point toward focusing on hip work. Take time before the lesson to think about what questions she might ask and work out the answers. Set the rest of the group up and then come to her in turn. She may want the count explained differently to suit her feet. Make sure she is well drilled in a hip move before you send her off travelling.

Noel loves to dance. While you are handing out paperwork, she is practicing her figure eights. Her moves are never perfect and her arms have their own ideas. But she will be the first to start moving once the music starts. Noel might take extra work to look polished in group choreography but she will be the star of the show. Try putting her in a subgroup where the others will follow her for a section. She is your greatest asset when it comes to free dancing because the others will follow her lead and explore the moves and room without being too self-conscious. She is a wonderful wild spirit, and you are lucky to get a Noel in your group.

Ollie is a wonderful transgender person. Just like all her classmates, she is exploring how her body works with the new movements and how it feels to be a belly dancer. Allow all your students time and space to work this through.

Paris has sadness in her eyes. She recently lost someone she loved. Although she wants to explore this exciting world of belly dance, she can't yet move on. Pick your free dance music carefully while Paris is in your class. She may not be ready to watch sad movies or dance from her heart yet. If she wants to tell you about her loss, tell her you are sorry. If she doesn't want to tell you, that is OK as well. Sadly, wherever you gather a large group of people you will have all kinds of experiences represented. Dancing from the heart is a way to bring all that experience out in a performance and share honesty and truth with an audience. One day Paris will dance in a way that will break your heart. It is your job as a teacher to take her down that path slowly and with little steps. She will appreciate you all the more for holding her hand on that journey.

You don't share a common language with Quinn, which means you need to be more visual in your explanations and more physical with your corrections. Try to learn how to say "good job" in her native language and use it often.

Robin is really young and shy. Her eyes light up when the music starts to play. She is quickly adopted by all the other students, who love to take her out to shows, hafla and workshops. She is always the first up on the dance floor and gets a great reaction from the crowd. Within a few weeks you hear from a friend that she has offered to undercut the house dancer at a local restaurant and has been seen dancing there in a tiny costume upstaging the paid dancer. You have a word with her and remind her that you need to work within a community. She thinks that you are trying to spoil her fun and restrict her creativity. Next thing you hear she is working in a club, specializing in floor work and offering private lessons. Robin is a reminder that we have to stay classy at all times and teach our beginner dancers to do the same.

Sky doesn't really have anyone close to her. She has work mates and some relatives but they all keep their distance. No one ever touches her or gives her a hug. Some of us have a very primitive need for touch. She will see you move another student and then ask for that kind of correction herself. If you are comfortable with being the main person to meet those needs for her, then go ahead and touch her arm while talking to her or give her a hug at the end of the lesson.

Toni accidentally flashes the audience during her first performance. You are horrified for her and try really hard to make her see that it could happen to anyone and you hope it won't put her off performing forever. For her second performance she arrives in a halter top and a see-through skirt. You tape her into her bra and lend her an underskirt. Unfortunately, she does quite a few turns and her skirt works its way up past her shoulders. When she arrives for her third performance in an outfit from an adults-only mail-order catalogue it is time to face the fact that she will always "accidentally" flash. You need to ask her to move on to another teacher's class.

Umut lost her father this week. Everyone in class knows that he has been ill. Today she has arrived in tears and she is probably still in shock. As a teacher you have a class to teach. You also have to set the tone for others and respect and acknowledge her pain. I would hug her, when she arrives, because I personally am the hugging type. I would speak to her about wanting to give her some circle time at the end of the session. I tell everyone to get on with the lesson in a businesslike manner before checking that my music is upbeat and I don't have anything unsuitable in the class material. I would then finish the lesson, five minutes early and ask if the others would like to stay and make a circle for Umut, if that is something she would like to share. However, I make it clear that it is optional for the others to stay or go. Then I would lead a simple meditation for Umut.

A born organizer, Val is a great team captain and she gets things done. She is not afraid to speak up in class and the others look to her to be decisive and vocal. She will bring in twenty-five options for troupe costume and voting slips to help keep things democratic. When you promise your class a demo of your first-ever solo, she will email you to remind you to bring the music. Val is a huge asset to any group and greatly speeds up all decision making, but don't let her push her views onto others or take over the running of the classes for you. Offer the quieter students the chance to express their views via the privacy of email. Be grateful for her offers of help and take what you need, but give the poor girl a day off from time to time.

After Whitney's first class you are pretty sure she won't be coming back. The class didn't seem to suit her. Maybe it was too hard, too easy, too long, or too short but she never smiled and she left without making eye contact. You are kind of surprised to see her back the second week, and then the third and the fourth. By the fifth lesson you know what it is she doesn't like about the class, because she told you. Whitney tut-tuts when you introduce a new move, rolls her eyes when you revisit an old one and generally pulls energy out of the class. You rewrite your term plan four or five times and come to the conclusion you are a terrible teacher. Ten years later, Whitney is still coming to class and looking disappointed in you, but now she does four classes a week and she lights up when she performs. When she comes off the stage she tells everyone what a terrible job she did.

Xandra changed class because she didn't like her old teacher. You are the best teacher she has ever tried. She writes nice things about you online. She attends only three of your lessons; then you see nice things she has written about another local teacher. You know she told her new classmates that you are terrible. Don't let it upset you.

Yasmin and Abbie have been best friends since they met on their first day at school. They went to college together and had babies at the same time. They talk to each other constantly, and it's becoming disruptive to the class. They love spending time together and their joy is contagious, but it's also a bit hard to get any teaching done. You can try to talk to them about it, but don't crush their joy. Teachers have been telling them to stop chatting since they were four, so just keep with the pattern. They happily accept the role of naughty schoolgirls and bring character to your class; just make sure your voice is heard and the other dancers don't resent their taking up too much of your time.

Zee books a course with you because her local restaurant wants a new belly dancer and they have promised to book her if she takes a few lessons. Take the time to let her know that although you may not be able to get her to performance level in just ten weeks, you are impressed with her commitment and ready to work with her. Assign her homework each week to drill key moves and to learn the classic performance tracks. Suggest other teachers she can learn from locally and give her a list of DVDs and music to order. Send her to workshops and shows. Zee may discover that performance-quality belly dance is tougher than she first thought, or she may surprise you with her hard work and focus.

SETTING UP A BUSINESS

Every part of the world has different rules about how to set yourself up as a business, but you will also find yourself surrounded by people who have done this before you, so look for help. Search for your local chamber of commerce or women business leaders group. Ask your hairdresser or taxi driver, your chiropractor and the café owner for advice. Many towns also run short courses on how to set up your business, so take advantage of these. Even if you are planning on only working for a gym or the local adult education organization, it is worthwhile setting up a business or becoming a sole proprietor now, before you get asked to teach a workshop, sell coin belts, or tour the world. Setting up a business should not be complicated, but it may take some time and involve some red tape; perhaps you need to place a classified ad in a newspaper, or send off eight passport photos or hand deliver a form to an office that is open only from 10 a.m. until 3 p.m. every third Thursday. Start this process now, so you never need to try and do it in a rush.

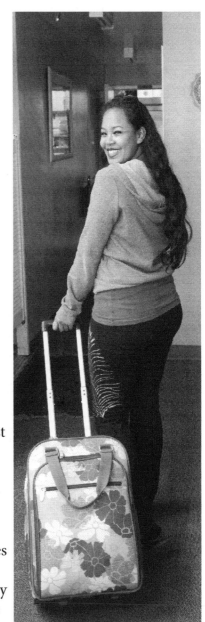

Perhaps the most fun to be had in setting up a business is choosing the name. Go for something that is easy to say and easy to read and tells new customers about your business. Most sole proprietors simply use their own name, but if you are using a dance name, do an extra sanity check. Your dance name may sound beautiful in the restaurant where you dance, but to another segment of society it may be the name of a toilet bowl cleaner. You do not want to be listed in the local telephone directory as a cleaning company. Test out any puns or joke names on people you know from outside the belly dance community. Also remember that you may be limited by this name for a very long time. If you have a tendency to change your dancer name or move around the country, you don't want to be stuck with "Jaida of Johnstown Belly Dance."

Practical Tip:
Find out about courses and local mentor groups willing to help with setting up your business.

SIMPLE ACCOUNTING

Accounting may be something you are already an expert in, or it may be new to you, but it is essential and important that you start from day one. The most basic form of accounting is the two-column system. You can do this on a sheet of paper or set up a simple table on your computer or with an app on your smartphone. The first column is your income; the second is your expenses. At the end of the year (or each month, if you'd like to stay on top of things), simply add up each and subtract the second from the first to calculate your profit (or loss!)

Your income will be all the money you make through belly dance: the money you charge for class, for selling belts, and teaching or hosting workshops, and any other money that comes in. By the side of each entry in the first column, note the source and the date. You may also want to note whether it was cash or check.

The outgoing list is everything that you spend money on in order to do your job. This will include a lot of setup costs: buying everything for your bag; business and music licenses; stocking up on belts and music; buying extra shoes, sports bras, or yoga pants to teach in. As the year goes on, you will have regular expenses like room rents, business cards, advertizing, and workshops (continuing education). All of these need to be recorded; again, note what the payment was for and how you paid.

Depending on where you pay taxes, you can add anything that is important to your business. If your cell phone is essential to your business and you rarely use it for personal calls, then you can put your monthly bills in your expenses. If you feel that having fake nails is part of the lifestyle that attracts students to belly dance, then you can include your monthly trips to the manicurist.

You should speak to a tax expert to clarify the tax laws in your own area, but to begin with, keep a note of everything. Don't forget office supplies and business use of a car.

To be a belly dance teacher you will need to attend workshops and events. If you perform somewhere that you can promote your classes or your workshops and you have to buy a ticket on the door, keep that for your expense records. You can include the cake you bought for a potluck party where you performed, a new lipstick for performance makeup, a few hours in a parking garage and blank CDs to burn for dance accompaniment. All these things have probably been part of your hobby in the past, but now that you are in business, you need to keep the receipts, note the business purpose and enter them in your accounts.

It will be scary at first to see how much you spend on belly dance. In the past, belly dance was something on which you spent your disposable cash. Now that it is a business, many of these items become more essential. If your students are enjoying a veil term, it will be important that you take an advanced veil workshop to get enough inspiration to write them a complex choreography. When it was your hobby you might have looked at your finances before deciding to attend, but now you need to budget so that you have the money available to invest in developing your skills.

Some teachers are happy if their teaching covers the costs of offering classes and some workshops and events they want to attend. Others are looking to make a profit by the end of the year. Any business, from corner shop to dot-com, expects to have some loss in the first few years, so don't be disappointed if the initial outlay swallows up all chance of a profit. Don't feel you have to quit or raise your prices; trust in your teaching skills and keep focused on your retention and new students until things pick up.

In some countries the tax man will be happy to just see your two-column account sheets; in other places you'll need to also keep all your receipts. I find the easiest way to do this is to buy a cheap notebook at the beginning of the year and staple them in, one per page. I also make a note of the important parts of the receipt, as they have a tendency to fade. I keep it simple: "May 10, yoga pants, $20, Yogatogo." The receipt book is in addition to the two-column account sheets.

Your main income will come from classes. If you take cash at the door, counting it out can become one of the highlights of your week. Don't forget to take out your initial stock of bills for change and return it to your cash box. In addition to entering the total take for each class in my accounts, I also write it in my diary, just in case my computer crashes and I lose all my accounts. Keep notes to try and track patterns in your income. Some are fairly obvious, like having more new students in January and September when the school sessions start up again. Others take a long time to spot. I found my Wednesday classes were always smaller when England played football. Knowing this in advance can help you with your planning. Sometimes it is better to take a night off than try to run a class when the local Arabic nightclub is offering free drinks all night.

Practical Tip:
Take a look at a couple of simple accounting software options. Some come free with other software or as an app for your phone. Take a trip to your local stationery shop and see if you would prefer an accounting notebook.

ETHICS IN TEACHING

This can be a real minefield. What I have to offer here is by no means a complete discussion, nor are my observations going to apply in 100 percent of cases, but my intent is to help you, as a new teacher, avoid some of the classic mistakes that can upset other dancers and teachers you may be hoping to work with.

Don't undercut, either in your performing or your teaching. Your local area will have a fairly standard range of fees for everything you will be doing, and it's best to stick to that price. You do not need to price yourself cheaper because you are new to dancing or teaching. There are some variations in class prices; for example, a city center dance studio may be charging twice the room hire rate that you'd pay at your town's rec center, but it should also attract twice as many students. You should be able to set your pricing very close to that of others working locally and still make a living. If you can't find a local belly dancer to compare fees with, try to find someone who works in a similar location: look at average house prices, wages, and unemployment levels. It is also worth comparing your prices with those of yoga teachers, judo classes, pole dance, or other classes in your location. Keep in mind, some gym classes are cheaper if you are a member; add annual fees and monthly dues to your calculations.

> ## Practical Tip:
> Find out the per-hour price of belly dance classes in your area, or a similar area. Calculate hall rental costs and add in 15 percent for insurance and licenses. How many students will you need to break even? This is a very rough calculation, but it works as a starting point.

Don't teach other people's material (without permission or credit). This is not black-and-white, of course; there's a spectrum. At one end, it is clear that no one can copyright a figure eight; at the other, it should be obvious that the dancer who wrote choreography owns it. In between are lots of ideas, combinations, concepts, and sayings that are strongly linked to certain dancers.

If you buy a DVD that gives the user permission to perform the choreography on it at events where you are not paid (like the local hafla), I would still suggest that you change it to suit your dance strengths, and of course credit the dancer who wrote it. It does not give you permission to teach it to others. The producer of the DVD would like you to suggest to others who like your performance that they buy the DVD.

You might like a combination (a short sequence of moves) and go on to use that in a new choreography or teach it as an example of how to dance in a particular style. In that case, you should credit it to the DVD, again suggesting that students make a purchase. It would be best to alter the combination in some way.

You could introduce it with language like "I learned this combination from a DVD of Miss Amazing Dancer, but she tends to power a turn from this hip rotation; I like to complete the rotation and then do a slower walk-through turn, which suits the slower music I have chosen." Or perhaps "You need to watch Mr. Shimmy! He does this amazing thing where he layers a really strong walk with a huge hip shimmy and these little wrist rotations. Try it; see how it works only if you keep a strong posture . . ." Your students will respect you for being knowledgeable in your subject and for bringing them amazing new inspirations.

If you take a workshop, ask about performing any choreography taught there. Teachers have different views on this. Again, any ideas or combinations that you find yourself using or adapting should be credited in class, and you might consider inviting the teacher to come to your area to teach a workshop. If you learn a new style of dance or get lots of inspiration from a workshop, it is good manners to describe any performance that comes from that work as "inspired by Miss Specialist." Not only does that help her get her name noticed, it also shows that you have studied with a master teacher.

Teachers often share short video clips, which can be fun and very inspiring. It doesn't take long to send a teacher a quick message asking if you can use her work in one of your lessons; usually they are very happy to hear from you. Again, be quick to give credit. In the same way that an art teacher might pick a picture by a master to inspire the class, you can find a clip you love, send it to your students, and ask them to reinterpret it as a holiday project or homework. By showing them that you are always learning, you can lead by example, helping them to explore the wonderful world of belly dance.

Don't upstage other dancers or dance students in performance settings. We all love to see other dancers perform or go out to restaurants where there may be dancers. Sometimes those dancers may not be very good, and though as teachers we would love to help them improve, a performance setting is not the time or place, and our input may not be welcome. If the dancer is a beginner, you may crush her journey of improvement. If the dancer is a world-famous performer in a style you may not know, you could end up looking foolish for suggesting she take more lessons to, say, tidy up her out-of-control arms.

If the performer pulls you up to dance, it is polite to refuse at first and then to stand to one side with a few basic hip drops while the performer remains the star. Of course, the performer may know who you are and want to show off your friendship, in which case you can echo her moves for a while, throw in one of your own, but then back off with some applause and let her finish the set.

If the performer liked how you danced, she may well come up to you later and ask for your business card. If she asks you about your lessons, you can tell her, but don't bring the subject up yourself. You can always ask for her card in the hope that she'll ask for yours in return, or ask if you can find her on a social network site.

If the restaurant owner asks you about performing, tell them that you will give your card to their house dancer. Sadly, in my experience the owner is often more interested in the possibility that you will dance for a lower fee than in engaging the best dancer for his guests. You don't have to tell the house dancer about that conversation unless you already know each other well. Short-term restaurant bookings are not worth the chance of ruining a friendship with a local dancer. She is much more likely than any restaurant owner is to connect you with work and students.

Offer to host workshops, not to teach them. Offering to teach a workshop for another teacher is a belly dancer snub. The subtext of that conversation is that you consider yourself the better/more interesting/more specialist teacher. It is similar to contacting a restaurant, offering to bring the chef dinner, and charging her for it. It is assumed that once you have been teaching for a year or so, you will have a good solid workshop planned, and you can announce that on your website and through social networks. If other teachers believe that you have something different to teach, a strong skill or style, they will contact you and book you to teach in their area. If you are not getting booked, you may have to promote your website, perform at more events attended by workshop hosts, or just be patient. Workshop hosts have their pick of hundreds of dance teachers who are willing to teach the basics, like veil choreography; instead, strive to create and market a workshop that will be unique.

There are exceptions to these cautions about contacting others and asking them to host you. If you are travelling to a different country or three or four hours from your usual area, you may want to contact a dancer you already know in that area and ask her about available opportunities. If a dancer has hosted you before, you can assume that she will be willing to do so again. Also consider contacting large events to find out about their booking procedure. One good workshop at a large festival can set a dancer up with bookings for years to come.
Instead of looking for others to host you, look into hosting other teachers who can provide your students with workshops that expand both your and their knowledge. Bringing a high-quality teacher to your area also helps promote you as part of the backbone of a thriving belly dance scene in your area.

Don't sell music unless it is yours to sell. Years ago, when it was hard to buy belly dance music, teachers would copy their vinyl to cassette or take a trip to Egypt and buy up a suitcase full of bootleg music. This has long since become unnecessary; now there is a huge range of music available through traders at events or online. I like to check that the music tracks I will be using for class choreography are available on a major website for a small payment and send my students a link to buy the album. Musicians are artists too, and they deserve to be paid. No one can complain about buying a single track to help them practice when the price is so affordable. I have been asked hundreds of times if I would copy a CD for a student, and I have always said no. It may be boring to keep repeating the same conversation, but your students will respect you for being very clear about not breaking the law.

Don't attend another teacher's class on the sly so that you can teach the same class. There is a fine line between continuing your education and taking a class on Monday that you turn around and teach later in the week. This process is known as "teaching on," and it works like a pyramid scheme. If you feel you don't have enough material to teach a class, then consider finding a mentor. If you want to continue with a class or change to a new class to aid your learning, then let your teacher know that you are now teaching class too. A strong online presence can be useful for this. Send your teacher a link to your website or give her your business card, and there won't be any confusion. Again, make sure you credit your teacher for any work inspired by her and link to her on your website. It is perfectly normal for teachers to also take classes with others; just make sure everyone knows about your change in status.

There's no sense in pretending that you woke up one morning as an expert in belly dance. When creating your website, include a nod to your first teachers, even if they weren't that wonderful. It is easy to pretend that you learned belly dance from a master teacher or a famous name whom you just happened to meet while walking past her workshop. Even if your first teacher messed up your posture, taught you that belly dance dates back to the prehistoric prostitutes, and called a shimmy a "jiggle," she still passed on a love of belly dance and deserves a mention in your life history. Belly dancers have a long memory; someone will remember you turning up in your jeans and trying to jiggle at the back of the room all those years ago.

Don't overdo the marketing at other people's events. It's good to have a business card on you at all times. It is also nice, if you are running an event, to set out a table where others can place business cards and flyers, but don't take it too far. Don't announce halfway through a workshop that you are starting teaching weekly classes soon. Don't hand out your business cards to the father of the bride at another dancer's wedding. And don't steal the sign-in sheet as a way to harvest email addresses! Many social network groups will happily accept an ad at the beginning of the year or once a week, but keep in mind that some of your contacts will also be members of multiple sites. If they get your ad all day, every day, you may seem desperate. Always apologize for duplicate posts and try to keep your own mailing lists tidy and up-to-date.

Get liability insurance and encourage dancers, teachers and studio owners you work with to be insured too. Insurance protects you as well as your students. Quotes can be obtained over the internet or via your usual broker, and you can cover not only your classes, but end of term parties and shows with one policy. To give you a rough idea of cost, my current insurance is equivalent to sixteen students attending a one hour class (16 x $15 = $240). In addition to public liability insurance, consider how you would pay your bills if an injury prevented you from teaching for any length of time. When teaching a workshop or hosting another teacher, have an open conversation about what insurance you both have and make sure all the angles are covered.

HANDOUTS

The following are example handouts that I have used for my classes. Please feel free to copy, adapt or disregard them as you wish. You may find that they inspire your web site or emails rather than a paper copy.

WELCOME TO THE BEGINNERS CLASS

Teacher's Name (Insert Your Name Here)
Website • Email • Telephone

Class schedule dates & locations

Thank you for signing up for the belly dance class. I look forward to teaching you all about the wonderful world of belly dance!

Themes for this Group — In class we will be covering some basic moves and, toward the end of the sessions, travelling across the floor with them. We will also have the chance to discuss some of the different types and styles of Middle Eastern dance, folkloric dance (including Ghawazee), Al Jeel (modern pop), drum work, veil dance, American Tribal Style (ATS), classical, and baladi (urban). I will try to introduce a number of different music artists to you and show you a variety of different costumes. One of the best things about belly dance is that it has something to suit everyone; it will be my aim to help you find your style and gain the confidence to dance with it. If you find a particular step doesn't suit you, don't give up; leave it for a few weeks, then try again. Some of the steps we will try use muscles we don't normally use or need a flexibility we don't all have. Given time, your body will adjust and the moves will come more easily. Having said that, belly dance should be relaxing and natural. The main thing to remember is to enjoy yourself!

What to bring — There are a few things it would be useful for you to bring to class each week. First, you need to wear something loose and flexible. You will find dancers in our classes in everything from jogging pants and T-shirt to full bedlah (two-piece with beads and sequins). I am happy for you to wear whatever you feel comfortable in. I tend to have my tummy out often, because I find it helps students to see the moves more clearly. During the warmer months it can be more comfortable to wear a crop top, but again, it's a matter of personal preference. All tummies are acceptable in my classes. A good sports bra is essential for most women, but anything tight or form-fitting on the tummy or hips (including jeans) could be restrictive and is best avoided. Not all floors are clean, so most students prefer to wear soft-soled shoes (like ballet pumps). A length of material tied around the waist helps us keep the focus of the moves, or I have some coin belts you can purchase. You will also need to bring some drinking water, and you are welcome to take a water break whenever you need one. If you have a good reason for keeping your phone turned on, please let me know and we can keep the phone out where you can hear it ring; otherwise, please turn all phones off during class. I would also be grateful if you could start a class folder to keep the various handouts in and bring it to class each week. You can get extra copies of handouts via email or in class.

Your teacher — Hello, my name is Sara Shrapnell, and I will be teaching you to belly dance. I have more than fourteen years' teaching experience and twenty years of dancing belly dance, before which I trained in both ballet and disco. I regularly perform at weddings, parties, haflah, and stage shows. I have written for Taqasim and Mosaic magazines, and I am a member of Mosaic Arabic Dance Network in the UK, MEDCA in the United States, and a number of internet-based groups. In 2000 I qualified with both City & Guilds (national certificate in teaching adults) and Al Kahira School of Middle Eastern Dance (ASMED; subject training); I then went on to mentor others. I am fully insured to teach adults. You are welcome to discuss anything dance-related with me either after class or via email: LetsBellyDance@Hotmail.com. Please also find me on my social network sites. (This is an example of the text I use, obviously you will include your own bio here.)

For your safety — You will be asked to complete a waiver form; should your health change during the term, this needs to be updated when you return to class. Please make sure you know about the fire exits, and keep bags and coats away from the dance floor (or in lockers where available.)

What you can expect: —Joining our classes should be like joining a club, where you can have as much or as little involvement as you want. Four times a year you should receive a copy of my e-newsletter, Shimmy News, which is produced to keep you up-to-date with what is happening within our group. You will also be asked if you would like to join any of our email groups, which are for either up-to-date information or discussion outside class time. Or you can keep in touch via Facebook groups for each class. In addition, there will be handouts on costume retailers, music recommendations, websites, and magazines. Spare copies of these handouts are often available in class, and you can help yourself any time.

Belly dance is a performance art, and as such I organize a number of events each year where the dancers can get some performance experience. None of these are compulsory, although they should all be fun. Those not performing are encouraged to support these events, which are a fantastic opportunity to see new skills performed as well as the popular costumes and styles. We also invite visiting teachers to teach workshops locally, and we organize trips to performance and workshops in other areas.

What we expect from you — It is important that you confirm your place on a course at least a week in advance. This helps me with planning and also saves time on the first day of a course. You can notify my office of a planned absence; an unplanned absence can be emailed, called in to the phone number above, or left through the main office. Please arrive on time; it's considerate to other students, and the warm-up is most important to your general health. If you are struggling with a step, move to the side of the room and ask for help from your teacher. But remember that the occasional step in the wrong direction is perfectly fine! I expect all of us to work as hard as we wish at each lesson. I am happy to give "easy" and "hard" versions of each move, but as a general rule the slower and more controlled the movements, the harder they are on the muscles. Fast travelling moves are more aerobic. Breathing should always be regular and relaxed, and nothing should ever hurt. Try to maintain good posture for the whole of the class and throughout all your practice. The more you practice, the better you will become.

Moving up — Those in a beginners group should expect to move up to something for intermediates after about twenty to thirty weeks, depending on practice time. A full list of the classes I provide is on the website and in Shimmy News.

SAMPLE WAIVER

Teacher's Name (Insert Your Name Here)
Website • Email • Telephone
Class Dates & Location

Participants remain responsible for their own health and fitness during all belly dance classes and workshops and while onsite. It will help your teachers to know a little about your current health. Please read this list and check off any factors that have affected you in the recent past or may affect you currently:

- Fainting, dizziness, low blood pressure
- Back pain, joint pain, neck or head injuries
- Asthma, shortness of breath, chest pains
- Allergies to anything you may find in the dance studio or severe allergies to anything
- Heart condition
- Surgery within the last year
- Serious illness within the last year
- Pregnancy within the last year, or planning for pregnancy
- General feelings of being unwell, including but not limited to: recent cold or flu, chest infection, chronic fatigue, compromised immune system, D&V (Diarrhea and vomiting), change in diet, change in fitness routine, change in sleep patterns
- Long-term illness or disabilities

Please feel free to speak to me privately or use the space on this form to note any problems. I would prefer to have your permission to disclose any health information in an emergency, as I feel appropriate.

Please sign and date below to say that you feel fit and able to take part in dance and fitness classes. It is your responsibility to inform your teacher if you have a change in your health. If you are at all worried, please seek medical advice. I am more than happy to speak or write to your doctor personally.

Signature ....Date......................

Waiver continued

I, ...
agree to take full responsibility for my own body, belongings, and welfare during dance class.

I will not hold (Insert Your Name as Instructor) nor any substitute teacher responsible nor liable for any injuries or loss sustained while attending classes, or in the class venue, or while practicing, performing, or partying.

I will take care of myself and my belongings (including my car) while on site.

I will be responsible for any property that I damage while on site.

I will take care when practicing dance at home and have taken note of the instructions to warm up before practice and to monitor my posture to help make movements safe at all times.

I understand that during a dance class the teacher may use touch as a teaching method, and I give (Insert Your Name as Instructor) and her substitute teachers permission to touch me while other people are present in the room, help me with costume changes, and talk about body parts using both common and scientific terms.

I am over eighteen.

Signature. . . . . Date. . . . .

Your Copyright Statement Here

Please get legal advice before completing and handing out your waiver.

PREPARING FOR PERFORMANCE

Teacher's Name (Insert Your Name Here)
Website • Email • Telephone
Event Date & Location

I am excited about sharing your first belly dance performance with you! I hope that this hand-out answers most of your questions and helps you feel confident. If you have any other questions, please email me any time at [email address].

About two weeks before your performance:

Find a costume – As this is a first performance for this group, we will keep the costumes very simple. You will need black clothing with your colorful coin belt, a colorful tube of fabric (like a cami top with the straps tucked away), and a big, colorful flower in your hair. The flower does not have to match your belt or tube skirt, but all should be bright and cheerful. Your clothing should be a combination of a floor-length dress or yoga pants or floor-length skirt or long leggings and/or T-shirt or cami or short dress over leggings. All in black. Necklines can be anything you like except strapless. Halter neck and one shoulder must be over a sturdy black bra. Practice your turns with the flower in your hair and glue it to a headband or hair clip if necessary. For this costume we are looking for a combination of uniform and personality!

Find your makeup – Strong pigment is more important than pricing, so don't feel you have to spend a lot of money. Look through your old makeup for bits and pieces that you rejected for being too strong, as they may be perfect for your performance. You will need: liquid foundation (your daytime or evening one will be fine for this setting), concealer (only if you usually use it), and very red lipstick. Brown or orange reds can look yellow under lights; purples and blue reds tend to turn black. Tell the cosmetic clerk that it is for a performance and she won't try so hard to talk you into something more daytime. Your everyday rosy blush, black eyeliner (liquid or pencil), and a trio of eye shadows including a very dark, a medium, and a very light (or you can blend your own with colors you already have), false eyelashes, and an eyebrow shaper. Do not buy a whole new makeup kit!

About a week before your performance

Get your eyebrows done — Shaped eyebrows change the whole look of your face. Personally, I like the threading ladies in the mall. Eyebrow shaping is always painful the first few times, but you will love your new look, and you can maintain it for months yourself. Do it a week early so you have time to get to know your new face.

Buy nail polish — If you don't normally wear nail polish then it is good to practice ahead of time. Any bright color is fine, but for this performance I would like your toes to match your fingers.

Perfect your dance — Make sure you know every moment of your dance. Practice on your own at least once a day. Print out your notes and put them on the fridge or as a marker in your bedtime book. Read it just before you go to sleep.

Invite someone — Performing is so much more exciting when you can share it with a friend or family member. Please bring someone along to look after your bags, take your photo, and tell you how wonderful you danced.

On the day of your performance

Get lots of sleep — Don't be nervous. I am very confident that your performance will be wonderful.

Eat something — Eat your normal food plus a couple of healthy snacks. We may be eating late, and you don't want to be worried about being hungry and finding food to ease the pangs. Good proteins help keep the energy levels up all day.

Manicure your nails — Allow plenty of time to paint your nails. This is one job that can't be rushed or done while multitasking. Make a phone call or watch TV for an hour and you will avoid nail polish drama.

Pack your bag — Double check the packing list, and if you some spares, put them in the car.

Check your directions — The parking lot is a bit tricky to see, but it's easy to go around the block if you miss it. Ensure you have change for any parking lot fees or attendants.

Put on clothes that don't leave marks — Some dreses, skirts and pants, will etch lines onto your body. Elastic waistband and bra strap lines can take an hour to fade, so swap into comfy clothes a couple of hours before you leave the house. A maxi dress is nice to arrive in, or yoga pants and a T-shirt. Try out a T-shirt with a built-in bra. Although I could never jog in one, I find they are fine for driving to the venue.

Here is a list of a few things to bring with you to the show

Your music — Someone in your group needs to bring a spare copy. Mark with your name, the name of the piece you want to dance to, and its running time.

Your makeup — Good strong colors, lots of layers; put most of it on at home. Have a practice a few days before. Take a photo in poor light and strong light to see how it looks.

Hair products — Prepare your hair at home beforehand. Please, no sprays in the venue.

Your costume — Check it for stress and strains. Make a list for the entire outfit for each number you are appearing in, including skirt or pants, top or dress, belt, and veil, shoes (or wet wipes for feet), necklace, earrings, and extras (stick, headdress, zills, flower), and underwear (matching); note the music for each number on that costume list.

A spare costume — You might end up clashing with someone – or worse still, spilling food down yourself. Bring a few basics you are comfortable dancing in – a spare skirt, top, and belt. If you are dancing in a group number, bring any suitable spares, so you can help out anyone who has forgotten anything.

A cover-up — So you don't show the audience your costume before you appear on stage. Please, out of respect for other dancers, no jangling coin belts when you're not performing.

Drinking water — Don't bring drinks into a changing room. That is how accidents happen.

Snack — Depends on when you are dancing and how your tummy settles. Maybe some mints or an energy bar.

A sewing kit — Bring thread to match your costume, already on a needle.

Medical supplies — It's useful to have plasters/self-adhesive dressings, headache tablets, and tissues in your bag.

Camera — It's always polite to ask a dancer before you photograph her (the flash can be really blinding in a dark room). Action shots are almost impossible to get, so take time during the break to gather your group together and take posed photos.

Do Not Bring — strong perfume, spray glitter, or hair spray, all of which damage costumes and trigger allergies and asthma in other dancers. Be respectful.

On the night:

The show starts at 7:30 p.m. Please arrive as close to 7 as possible. Check the running order and report to the stage manager or let me know you are on site.

Alcohol before a performance is never a good idea, no matter how tempting!

Dressing rooms are very small, so either keep your costume with you or store it neatly. Please give priority in the changing rooms to those who have to perform early in the evening.

It is helpful if you can put on most of your makeup at home. Liquid foundation can take some time to dry, so put that on half an hour before the rest of your makeup. Do not put on your makeup near other people's costumes.

You should be able to watch most of the show before and after your performance from the back of the room. Please bring a simple cover-up (veil, large shirt) to put over your costume while out in the audience, and remove anything jingly.

Two numbers before yours, make sure you have your costume on and someone to mind your handbag/purse (and your children). At the end of that number, gather in a corner and check that all members of your group are present. Get warmed up and make sure you know where you are standing to start and what order you are going on. Please allow the performer before you to leave before you go onto the stage area. You will probably not be announced at this venue. Once on the stage, hold your opening position until the music starts – this will feel like forever. At the end, hold your position for a count of five to make sure of a good photo, and lead off in character.

When you're done, before you go back to watch the rest of the show, make sure your bag is packed away. If you would like to stay and enjoy the open floor after the show (and I think you should!), please make sure you are wearing something slightly different from your costume. Swap your T-shirt, put on a bright dress, swap out your coin belt. Think quick change, but this is the time for you to be an individual. Some dancers spend the whole night in their costume, but I would prefer it if you didn't.

Please remember you can email me at any time. If you can't make it, please email me or phone me as soon as you know so that we don't try and bump your number until later in the evening. Oh, and have fun!!

Packing list:

- Top half of your costume
- Bottom half of your costume
- Belt
- Shoes/wet wipes
- Underwear
- Hair decoration
- Jewelry
- Props
- Zills
- Makeup
- Hair products/pins
- Cover-up
- Music
- Directions
- "Going home" underwear
- "Partying" clothes
- "Going home" clothes
- Pins/toupee tape/sewing kit
- _____
- _____
- _____
- _____
- _____
- _____
- _____

SAMPLE TIME LINE FOR OUR NEXT PERFORMANCE

Saturday night

7:30 — Perform
7:00 — Arrive at venue
6:00 — Be ready to leave home; play your music in the car
5:45 — Load car, check maps
5:30 — Eat your snack
5:00 — Put on makeup and travelling clothes
4:30 — Set hair, assemble makeup
4:00 — Pack bags, shower
3:45 — Ring me by this time if you can't make it tonight
3:00 — Relax, paint your nails
2:30 — Make sure you have eaten and prepare a snack for later

Friday night

- Get lots of sleep
- Check your packing list and make any last-minute repairs to your costume
- Check that your phone and camera are charged
- Practice applying your makeup and false lashes
- Check that your music works on a CD player or iPod
- Have one last practice

Thursday

- Dress rehearsal; please bring your complete costume (including props and head dresses) and put on your makeup
- Plan your route for Saturday; if carpooling, call or email to confirm
- Review your music
- Bring any quesitons or problems to class

This week

- Invite your family and friends.
- Buy tickets.
- Check your makeup bag and see if your nail polish has expired, solidified or dried out in the bottle.
- Practice!

PERFORMER/TROUPE AGREEMENT

Teacher's Name (Insert Your Name Here)
Website • Email • Telephone

Thank you for agreeing to dance with me at our next event. The following are a few points I would like you to consider before attending your first performance with me.

Please read a copy of the booking form that I send to prospective customers. Let me know if you have any comments or suggestions.

I will let you know what I would like us to perform at each event with as much notice as possible. If you feel that you are not ready to perform a particular dance at an event, please let me know during the planning stage; we can arrange more practice time, or you can come along and support us instead.

This performance group has not been set up to provide financial profit for anyone, nor can we cover costs you may incur. Most of the work we are offered is for charity or for other dance studios and offers no fee. If I do secure a fee for an event, or if we get tips on the night, I will split it, with half going to the costume account and half to be shared among the dancers who perform at that event. The costume account will be used to provide essentials for the group, with each expenditure being discussed with the group beforehand; in previous years it has covered the shipping on our group orders.

Choreographies taught to the group remain my property. You may not perform or teach my choreography without my permission.

Please commit to a performance as early as possible after we get the booking. If you miss practice, other dancers may be asked to fill a space. Should you commit to a performance and not attend practice, your place may or may not be cut, at my discretion.

By committing to perform with our group, you agree to the following:

• Dancers are expected to obtain or purchase suitable costumes and keep them well maintained at their own expense.

• Dancers may be asked to wear a costume that doesn't suit them, dance a move they dislike, or style their hair or wear shoes to match the group. These things are part of fitting in with a troupe. While I encourage the individual, I also encourage the group as a whole to have a uniform look; this requires reasonable adaptation from all of us. Adaptation will be considered unreasonable when more than half of the group disagrees with a costume idea. In this case the idea will have to be changed. New dancers joining the group are expected to accept the costumes and choreographies already used by the group.

• Dancers are expected to be professional at all times while representing me or the studio. This includes but is not limited to: not drinking before a performance, while in costume, or while in a studio T-shirt; not discussing other dancers while at events; not using bad language or being overly loud while at events; not taking video or photographs of dancers without full permission; not posting video/music/photos online without all permissions; and not posting negative comments about events on social networking sites.

• Should I have worries about safety, payment, or an event being bad for the studio's name, all members will remove themselves from the venue as soon as possible and leave any necessary discussion for a later time and place.

• To be professional, we need to arrive at the venue on time with all our costuming and music. Please check these things before you leave the house, and bring spares if possible. You are responsible for any purchases you may need, such as CDs, props, and costume.

• Should you be offered work as a dancer or for our group at this event, please refer the customer to me. You may accept solo work that comes through other sources (friends, work, family), but please keep yourself safe, and consider taking a friend with you.

• Tips offered can be accepted with good grace at the discretion of each performer, although it should be added to the pot to be divided as above. I do not encourage dancers to intentionally seek tips, or to accept them in any other way than in the hand, showered overhead, or in the "hat."

• In the event of a problem during a performance, dancers should continue to the best of their abilities, maintaining good posture and a wonderful smile. Soloists should be able to expect other dancers who are offstage to handle problems for them. In the case of a group dance, the group leader should move to the front center of the stage, giving the others the chance (by clearly marking basic moves) to follow or to frame (by confidently performing solo moves or a taqsim). If one of the backing line feels the need to contact the organizer or stage manager, she should leave the stage "in character" to do so. When in doubt, smile and figure eight, hands on bum.

• Dancers are responsible for their own transport to events and any parking fees and entry fees. Some events also ask dancers to bring a dish or to purchase photographs or video footage of the event. Where possible, I will try to make you aware of these costs ahead of time and to negotiate a group discount.

Thank you again for agreeing to perform and represent my studio at this event. I am delighted that you are going to join our team, and I know we are going to have lots of fun at the events I have lined up for us. If you have any questions at any time, do not hesitate to contact me at the above number.

Your Copyright Statement Here

HANDOUTS AND CONTRACTS
FOR USE IN PREPARATION OF YOUR NEXT EVENT

Running your own event can be a wonderful experience, and one your whole dance commnity can enjoy. Lighten your load with preparation, forethought, and handouts. Your team of helpers will feel confident in their roles if you give them clear directions before the event. Here are samples of the forms and paperwork that I use for student haflas.

HELPERS HANDOUT

Event Title:
Date & Location:
Organizer Name:
Contact details on the day of event:
Contact details before the event:
First aider/emergency responder on the day:

Thank you for offering to help at our event. Without helpers like you, this event could not take place, and I am hugely grateful. Here are a few notes to help the event run smoothly:

Please be on site by 6 p.m. If you are going to be late, please call me before 4 p.m.; after that time my phone may be turned off, as I will be driving, but you can leave a message.

Setup is between 6 and 7 p.m. I will have copies of all contracts, handouts, and notices in my stationery box, which will be under the front desk. Please feel free to help yourself to anything you need. The venue has asked that we not use pushpins except on the notice board by the front desk. Please encourage smokers to use the bench by the parking lot only.

We have asked performers to arrive at 6:45 p.m. Please send them to the changing rooms. If they wish to keep seats, they may reserve only the back two rows.

We aim to open the doors to the public at 7 p.m. Please let the front desk know if you are not ready by that time.

The show will start at 7:30 p.m. We will keep a section of the seating near the lobby door for you to watch the show.

The show should finish around 9 p.m. I would like to thank you all publicly, so please be prepared to come onto the stage to be recognized.

We have the space until 10 p.m., and I would really appreciate your help in cleaning up and getting all the performers out of the building in time. Extra help is always needed to help the vendors pack up their vans, so please help if you finish your area early.

The following is a list of your responsibilities. Please let me know ahead of time if you feel you are unable to fulfill any of these.

Please let me know if you have any questions, and my thanks to all of you again for offering to help make this show such an enjoyable evening for all our guests and performers.

The following are a list of duty assignments and chores broken down by category. These lists are just suggestions, and the needs of your event and space will vary.

First aider/emergency responder

Please be onsite at 5:30 and stay until everyone has left.

Please bring your first aid kit and make sure your cell phone is fully charged.

Introduce yourself to all the other helpers.

You have a seat allocated at the back by the door to the changing rooms. Please keep your phone set on vibrate so that we can all call you at any point in the evening.

I hope your skills are not needed!

Thank you!

DJ

All the music is on one playlist and burned onto one CD.

Please check it on the night with a play-through and also for sound level.

There is a playlist called "Before and after" with soft music to welcome the audience in and to see them out.

The show playlist is called "Show."

After the introductions, please press Play. The music should play straight through.

Dancers have let us know whether they wish to start on stage or off. If on stage, please pause the music and give them time to get into position.

Thank you!

Treasurer

Please collect the float/cash box from me for the front desk and raffle.

Take the floats to the lobby.

Please put reserved signs on the seats by the lobby door for our helpers to see the show. I think we need ten.

Collect money every ten to fifteen minutes and place in marked envelopes in your bag.

At the end, collect all money and cash from the raffle area.

Please keep the money secure until Monday, when I can bank it.

Thank you!

Front desk

Collect the float/cash box from the treasurer. Familiarize yourself with the building layout (particularly restroom location).

Decorate the front desk with a tablecloth.

Lay out flyers about my classes (other teachers are welcome to add their flyers); please keep this looking neat.

Direct performers to the dressing room.

Open the main doors at 7 p.m.

Take tickets and send the audience through to the main hall.

Direct guests to restrooms, smoking area.

Will-call tickets will be in the stationery box; each will indicate whether already paid for.

Cash payments only, please.

We have twenty tickets to sell at the door. If more than twenty people turn up without tickets, we will have to turn them away. Please give them my apologies.

Please stay at the front desk for ten minutes after the performance begins and then keep an eye out for anyone coming in late.
Please say goodbye at the front door as the audience leaves.

Help with packing the vendors.

Thank you!

Master of ceremonies (MC)

Please check with me for changes in the running order.

I will send you a script by Wednesday; let me know if you see any mistakes.

Check with performers on how to pronounce any names you think may be difficult.

At 7:20 welcome the audience and give them a ten-minute warning. Promote the vendors and the raffle.

7:30, introduction.

Please be prepared to fill in should there be technical difficulties.

Approximately 9 p.m., thank-you speech.

After the audience has gone, please go to the changing rooms to thank the performers for me and help them pack up.

Thank you!

Stage manager

I will provide you with a running order and on/off stage instructions by Wednesday.

Please meet and greet the performers as they arrive in the changing room, show them the entrance we want them to use, and check their on/off stage starts and finishes.

Give them each a call time approximately ten minutes before their performance.

At 7:15 give the MC her call and check that your opening numbers are almost ready.

Give verbal calls at minus ten minutes and move each performer to the stage entrance with five minutes to their entrance.

Check with all dancers that they have all their props with them at minus five minutes.

If a performer can't be found or misses her cue, it is your call to cut or reorganize the running order. Please inform the MC and DJ of your decision.

Please gather all the dancers just before the finale so that they can come onto the stage for their thanks. Some may have moved to the seating at the back of the room.

Thank you!

Wardrobe mistress

Please pack your sewing kit, extra pins, mirrors, and toupee tape. I will provide you with a bag of skirts and veils that can be used as extra layers in case of costume malfunction.

Clear the smaller room and place tables around the edge. Allocate space to the performers for their bags and to hang cases.

Pin up signs. Running order signs should be placed on all four walls and on the outside of the door. Place copy of "Chaging Room Rules" on main door, and on supply table.

Make sure they all know you cannot watch their bags.

Stage manager's word is law, so communicate any changes and encourage dancers to be ready for their calls.

Make sewing or costume repairs as and when needed. Offer to help with quick changes.

Encourage the performers to keep the room neat and tidy.

Foster a calm and relaxed atmosphere.

At the end of the show, help the performers pack and load their cars.

Please keep a bag of any lost property; I will collect it on Monday.

Thank you!

Food boss

Please set up two long tables on the far side of the main hall and cover with tablecloths.

I will provide paper plates and cutlery.

Place paper plates, napkins, and cutlery on far right, main dishes in the center, and sweets and treats at the far end.

Reorganize dishes as they are added to the table to keep a neat display.

Encourage people to help themselves throughout the evening.

Keep the food looking fresh by clearing empty dishes and combining salads and cake plates as needed.

Collect used plates in a trash bag every half hour or so and place them outside the back door by my car.

Clear up at the end. Feel free to box up anything you want to take home. Everything else in trash bags by my car.

Thank you!

Vendor liaison

Please be at the venue at 5:30 to help unload and set up the vendors. I have asked some others to be there to help you.

The vendors can each have one long table along the back wall. I have spare tablecloths if they don't have them.

They can each have a clothing rack to one side of their table. They should be bringing their own racks.

Offer to fetch them food and water, but don't mind their stall for them.

The treasurer will have change if they need extra.

The vendors have offered me a discount. Please check to see if they have the veils we want; if not, I will take the discount in coin belts. Feel free to pick out some you think the group will like. I will give you cash to spend on my behalf. Please ask for a detailed receipt.

Please stay to help them to pack up. We have to be out of the venue by 10 p.m., so make sure they understand that and we all work toward getting their vans loaded for them.

Thank you!

Guest star assistant

I will give you our guest's telephone number on Wednesday. Please text her Saturday morning to see if she wants anything (food, drink). You may need to call in to the shop on your way to the venue. Hand in receipts to the treasurer, and I will pay you back on Monday.

Please set up the small meeting room for her: clear the tables and set up a mirror.

She may be running late because she has an earlier performance. Please let the stage manager know when she arrives.

Offer to help her change, introduce her to the stage manager, and reinforce the schedule with her.

Offer to bring her food or drink.

Accompany her to the stage entrance.

Thank her after her performance and help her to pack and load her car.

Thank you!

DANCERS' CONTRACT

Date & Location:
Contact:
Host:

Thank you for agreeing to perform at our next event. Here are a few notes about our show:

The show will be at 7:30 at the Town Hall on Market Square. Directions are attached. The nearest parking lot is behind the bus station; there will be a parking fee of around $10. You may find free parking on one of the side roads, but check signage. Performers can arrive any time after 6:30. We plan for the show to be over by 9:30.

We do have to charge everyone who attends, including performers, but we have a group discount of six tickets for the price of five. Tickets can be purchased online on my website or by mail to my PO Box address.

We have a small changing room available for performers. We ask that you remind your friends that it is not big enough for visitors. You are welcome to meet up with your guests in the large lobby area.

Each performance should be between four and seven minutes long and can be in any style. This is a family event that is open to the public, so we request no bad language, political statements, horror/gore or tiny costumes. We reserve the right to cut short any performance we feel could be offensive.

The venue will not allow open flames. The ceiling is very high, so other props will work nicely.

The stage area is twenty-seven feet wide and eighteen feet deep. The floor and back wall are black. Black costumes do not work well on this stage. Lighting will cover the whole area and will be set to a warming glow. Unfortunately, we don't have spotlights.

Please submit your music via email or mail by the end of this month, along with a signed copy of this contract. If we don't receive your music, contract, and ticket order, we will assume that you do not want a performance slot and will pass it on to a performer on our waiting list.

Performers' music choices will be accommodated on a first come, first served basis; the second person making a selection will be asked to select an alternative song.

The playlist will be prepared in advance by the event host. To be prepared for the extremely unlikely event of the music not playing, we ask that all performers bring a backup of their music on CD.

It is essential that you check in with the stage manager thirty minutes before your performance slot. If you do not check in, you will be cut from the show. We are unable to offer any refunds in this situation.

The team behind this event is not responsible for any loss or injury at the event. You perform at your own risk. We cannot look after your bags, car, or children during your performance.

Access to the stage is up a short flight of stairs. If you or anyone in your party is unable to climb stairs, please let us know in advance so we can make alternative arrangements for access.

There will not be an official photographer or videographer at this event. You are more than welcome to bring your own camera. The hosts will not be able to film or take photos of your performance, but you are welcome to make your own arrangements with audience members. The hosts are not able to prevent other attendees of the event/member of the public from capturing your image, nor can we be responsible for how this image is used.

If you are unable to attend the event after committing to a performance slot, please give the hosts as much notice as possible. My telephone number on the day will be:

Thank you again for offering to perform. I am confident that it's going to be a wonderful show, and I look forward to watching your performance.

Signature
Date

PERFORMERS WAIVER

Event contact:
Website:
Email:
Telephone:
Event dates & Location:

I will not hold the organizers of (insert event name here) responsible nor liable for any injuries or loss sustained while attending or performing at this event.

I understand that I have been asked to provide the music for my performance ahead of time and it is enclosed, or has been emailed.

I will be responsible for any property that I damage while on site.

My performance is suitable for family viewing.

I understand that if I am late booking or arriving my number may be cut and I cannot have a refund.

I understand that the organizers cannot be responsible for any video or photographs taken at the event nor how they are altered or distributed in the future.

I am over eighteen

Signature .... Date ....

Your Copyright Statement Here

Please get legal advice before completing and handing out your waiver.

CHANGING ROOM RULES

Thank your for performing at this event. Here are a few rules to keep everyone happy:
Please keep the changing room tidy, clean and quiet at all times.

- No food or drink in the changing room.
- No perfume or hair sprays, no incense or deodorant sprays, no air fresheners. No strong smells.
- No music or dancing in the changing rooms. If you want to listen to music, please use headphones.
- No phone calls. Please set your phone to vibrate and take calls in another part of the building.
- No mess. Please use the bins provided and keep your belongings packed in your own bag.
- No checking out other peoples stuff.
- No drama.
- No smoking.
- No photographs or video. Other people are changing.
- No stress. Please work on calming nerves, not creating them.
- In this room the wardrobe mistress' word is law.

Last Words

I hope you have enjoyed learning more about the role of the belly dance teacher and feel better prepared to guide others as they discover this beautiful art. We are privileged to have the opportunity to take our passion and turn it into our business. Good preparation will help your classes to be enjoyable and stress free for both you and your students. You will develop dancers who have strong technique, can improvise, know about culture and history, and reflect well on you as a teacher.

Always remember to tailor your choreographies to fit your students skills, and allow yourself the joy of watching them perform. Your dancers will help you strengthen your local dance community and spread your love of this dance further. You are now a link in the knowledge chain. Be generous, kind, and understanding as you nurture the next generation of dancers.

Having the opportunity to teach belly dance has been a huge blessing in my life, and I wish you that same blessing in yours.

Wishing you many happy years of dance teaching and performing,

SELECTED GLOSSARY OF TERMS USED IN THIS BOOK

Al Jeel – Egyptian or Arabic pop music that has developed from the influence of rock and roll from the 1970s to the present. Originally the music style of the upper class youth, but now it crosses all classes. Simple verses and catchy choruses mix traditional instruments with electronic and computer-generated sounds.

ASMED – Al Kahira School of Middle Eastern Dance. A UK-based training course for belly dance teachers.

ATS – American Tribal Style belly dance. A group-improvised dance style developed by Carolena Nericcio and her FatChanceBellyDance group, building on earlier work by Jamila Salimpour and Masha Archer. The style is influenced by a variety of dance styles from around the world. ATS is also sometimes used as an umbrella term to cover groups who have been inspired by or who perform in the style of ATS but use choreography or have deviated from the original key moves and cues. Some groups adapt the name to better describe their performance style, such as American Tribal Fusion or Tribal.

baladi (raqs baladi, raks balady) – This dance style developed as musicians from the rural areas moved to the cities in the early twentieth century, bringing the traditional tunes up-to-date with modern instruments (such as the accordion and saxophone). The term baladi is applied to many things in Egypt, from fashion to food; it can mean unsophisticated and unfashionable or homely and native, depending on the background of the speaker. Live baladi follows a structured plan: musicians improvise a mix of classic tunes and taqsim highlights, with call-and-response sections and a variety of tempos.

choreography – A preplanned dance in which the moves are set to music. Can also refer to the written plan or sketch or diagram from which the dancers can learn the dance.

combination or combo – A collection of moves planned to cover a short phrase, verse, or chorus in a musical performance. A choreography may be made up by a number of combinations.

drills – A single move or a small group of moves repeated in order to increase fitness or muscle memory.

drum pattern – A repeated set of drumbeats that form a phrase.

drum solo – A dance performed to music in which the drumbeat predominates and the dancer focuses on following the drumbeat for the majority of the dance.

dum and tak – A simple way for dancers to describe the two main sounds in drum solos. A dum is a strong beat made when the drummer's hand hits the center of the drum skin. A tak is a lighter hit made by the fingertips on the edge of the drum.

finger cymbals (zills, zils, sagat, sagaat) – Musical instrument made up of four metal disks worn two per hand and played to accompany the dancing. Zils is the Turkish word while sagat is the Arabic.

folk dance – The traditional dance of a country, region, or group of people, usually performed by someone from that culture.

folkloric – In dance, a style influenced by the folk dance of a country, region, or group of people.

free dance (improvisation) – A dance without a preplanned structure.

Ghawazee (Ghawazi) – The Ghawazee were a group of travelling dancers. A subset of the Dom, they were often wrongly referred to as gypsies. Their dancing captivated travelers from as early as the 18th century, who featured them in art and literature. Only a few Ghawazee remain, dancing in a style that has resisted the modern dance influences such as ballet.

gothic dance – a modern style of belly dance influenced by the gothic movement. It is dark, dramatic, and emotional.

hafla – An Arabic style party, where everyone is welcome to share food and dance together. Although haflaat is the plural I have used hafla, which is more common in belly dance circles.

improvisation – See free dance.

Khaleegi (Khaleggi, Khaleeji, Khaliiji)– A dance from the Persian Gulf. It is best known for the beautiful, embroidered, long dresses and the free-flowing hair of the dancers.

layering – Adding two or move moves together to get a more complex look; for example, adding a shimmy to a hip rotation. It can also mean adding moves on different body parts; for example, adding a shoulder shimmy to a walk.

mentor – A senior dancer, performer, or teacher who is willing to assist others in their development.

nay (ney) – A wood or bamboo musical instrument in the flute family.

Nubian dance – Folk dance of the Nubian people, who live in the north of the Sudan and the south of Egypt.

Saiidi (Sa-idi, Sa3idi) – An Egyptian folk dance style that originated in El Said, the part of Egypt centered around Luxor, often performed with a stick or cane. Saiidi is also used as the name for a drum pattern associated with that area.

shaabi (sha abi) – A style of pop or street music popular in Egypt. Originally rising out of the slums, it is widely played but retains a stigma from its early popularity with the lower-class youth.

sharp moves – Moves that match a percussive hit.

soft moves – Moves that fit with the melody in the music.

stick (raks el assaya, cane) – A length of wood or cane used by belly dancers. Originally a folk dance from the El Said area of Egypt, this dance combines dance moves with balances, twirls, and frames with the stick. Many dancers now use these skills to non-saiidi music.

tak – See dum and tak.

taqsim (taqseem, takseem, taksim) – A section of music in which one instrument is featured and takes the starring role. Mostly improvised, it may be a solo with a soft drum accompaniment or a passage in which that instrument dominates the rest of the orchestra. In some tribal circles this term also describes a dance move.

tempo – The speed of a piece of music, sometimes described as beats per minute (BPM).

transition – The movement that bridges two recognized moves or two sections of music.

tribal – An umbrella term used to cover a number of modern styles of belly dance, including ATS and those who are influenced by ATS and those who use ATS as a component in their fusion style of dance.

Tribal Fusion – Style of dancers who mix ATS with another dance style. Often we see Tribal Fusion as a mix of ATS-influenced dance with modern dance, Bollywood-influenced dance, belly dance, flamenco, or Turkish dance.

undulating – To rise and fall. In belly dance this is a softening of the knees followed by a rise onto the balls of the feet, a more subtle move than the demi-plié and relevé of ballet. In some belly dance circles it is also used for a body or tummy wave.

zagreet (zaghreet, zegreet, zaghroot) – Also known as a ululation, this is a loud noise created with a rapid tongue movement, usually done with a hand covering the open mouth. It has different meanings and uses throughout the Middle East, but is commonly used to replace a cheer or clap during belly dance performances in the USA.

zills (zils) – See finger cymbals.

Acknowledgments

I am grateful to my teachers, who fostered in me not only a love for belly dance but also a wish to share it with others. Tina Hobin made the dance feel exotic and worth the struggle. Afra Al Kahira saw my potential as a leader and taught me to be self-accepting and to always study more. Emma Pyke has always been on my team, balancing out my weaknesses and making dreams a reality. In addition, I would like to thank all of those who have taken the time to teach me in workshops or to host me at events, teach classes for me, and answer my questions online. Belly dance teachers give without expectation, and I am grateful for all I have received.

I would like to thank the wonderful team behind this book:

Dawn Devine listened to my ideas and instantly believed in me. She inspired and coached me through this process for which I am hugely grateful. Amongst other things she organized and directed the photo shoots, managed layout and proof reading and kept me motivated when the task seemed too great.

Alisha Westerfield inspired the tone and look of this book with her amazing belly dance photos. She has the artist's eye in the way she captures the essence of each dancer, and I am honored to have been given the chance to step in front of her camera.

Additional photographs were provided by Donna Ovenden, Jesse Stanbridge and members of the Shrapnell family. Chi Chan designed the beautiful cover.

Poppy Maya adds additional awesomeness to everything she touches. Thank you for all your thoughts, critiques, the original cover design concept, motivation – and the coffee.

I was honored to have the opportunity to work with Leyla Lanty who added her wisdom, particularly to the glossary. A self-proclaimed language geek she helped with Arabic to English and American spelling options.

Along with Poppy Maya, my early editors were Donna Stafford-King and Rebecca Blachford. Donna brought fresh eyes to the project just as she started the journey toward teaching, and I am hugely grateful for her input. I know she will be a fantastic teacher, and I look forward to seeing her students perform. Rebecca has been a wonderful support since the first workshop I taught and she attended back in the early days of the Celebrating Dance Festival. Over the occasional bottle of pink wine we have discussed our thoughts on teaching, belly dance skills, and how best to share them.

This book was edited by Kristi Hein of Pictures and Words, Washington, who instantly understood my voice and left it untouched even after converting the book to American English. The proof readers were Eset, Sholane and Dawn. All remaining mistakes are my own.

I was blessed with a wonderful team of models to work with on this book :

Angie	Nilima
April Moun	Nyki
Basinah	Penny
Ea Indigo	Poppy Maya
Dawn	Sadira - Lady Liquid
Eset	Safiyah
Jesse Stanbridge	Shalimar
Katrina Curry	Sholane
Melina	Sidahlia
Michelle	Uyen
Nadirah	

Of course, I must thank all my students, who have not only taught me about teaching belly dance but also supported me financially and with their wonderful feedback. Please excuse me if I have overlooked anyone. I would like to thank the ladies of Mersin, who taught me how to teach dancers who have a better skill set than I do; the Monday group from Tadley, where we found magic; the Dublin class, who have shown me fresh enthusiasm; the Tuesday night students from Reading, who came so far; the Pleasanton Tuesday night dancers and the daytime class, which is unexpectedly advanced level; the glorious Wednesday night group from Basingstoke; the laid-back Thursday morning class in Oakridge, who taught me how to adapt; the class in Alton, where the coffee and chats helped build my confidence as a teacher; the Fort Hill group in all its formations; the Friday morning class, where I met wise women; the Friday night class in Livermore, where I am learning to teach in American; and of course the Saturday class, who covered almost every single topic in twelve years of continuous lessons. Each class has its own character, and I have loved dancing with you all.

Finally, I must thank my husband, Kevin. From my very first lesson he has believed in me. First he believed that I could be a belly dancer; then he convinced me I could make a living as a belly dance teacher. Now he has allowed me the space and time to spend a full year of our lives on writing and editing this book. Without his support and encouragement, my belly dance journey would have stumbled at my first misstep. He is enjoying the pause before our next big project.

Made in the USA
Lexington, KY
11 March 2015